# DESIGNING YOUR
# GREAT LIFE

# BEFORE YOU START READING!

Scan this QR Code for a special and
personal message from Jason.
And a bonus, 45 page "deep-dive" eBook

Or go to:
http://wittmanent.groovepages.com/offer

# DESIGNING YOUR
# GREAT LIFE

*Time-Tested Prescriptions for a Life Worth Living*

JASON WITTMAN

Library of Congress Control Number: 2022932181

# Designing Your Great Life!
## ~Time-Tested Prescriptions for a Life Worth Living~
Jason Wittman, MPS, LAADC, CATC-IV

*Artful Graphics Press*
### Hollywood, California

*Artful Graphics Press*
Published by Artful Graphics Press, February 2022
Printed in the United States of America

ISBN Paperback: 979-8-9852295-0-9
ISBN Hardcover: 979-8-9852295-2-3
ISBN for Kindle: 979-8-9852295-1-6
Library of Congress Control Number: 2022932181

Editor: Shari Reinhart
Interior Designer: Charlyn Samson
Book Cover Designer: Charlyn Samson

**Publisher's Disclaimer**
The purpose of this book is to educate. The author and the publisher do not warrant that the information contained in this book is fully complete and shall not be responsible for any errors or omissions. Also, this book provides information only up to the publishing date, therefore, it should be used as a guide - not as the ultimate source. Readers of this publication agree that the author and publisher shall have neither liability nor responsibility to any person or entity with respect to any loss or damage caused or alleged to be caused directly or indirectly by this book.

# Contents

## Section 2—Laying the Foundation for Well-Being

# Acknowledgements

Because this book is a compilation of material that I developed over many decades of counseling and coaching experience, I am taking this opportunity to thank and acknowledge not only those who played a role in the making of this book, but also the people who were most influential in my development both professionally and personally.

To the major therapeutic influencers, teachers and mentors that shaped both my counseling approach and my life including; John Grinder, Ph.D., William Glasser, M.D., Milton Erickson, M.D., Stewart Emery, Genie Z. Laborde, Ph.D., Tony Robbins, Earnie Larsen, Bhagwan Shree Rajneesh, Michael Durst, Ph.D., Ellie Macklin, Ph.D., Leonard Altman, Bobby Hayden, and T. Merrell Shipherd, LCSW

To Coach David Buck, MCC, the guiding light of Coachville Center for Coaching Mastery, for introducing me to many of the concepts I utilize in my practice and that made it into this book..

To my friends and colleagues who assisted in the editing and beta-reading of this book; Dan Benton, Gary P., Stephanie Stolz, Ph.D., Bobbi Nassar, Ph.D., Anna Fussell, and especially, my editor Shari Reinhart.

To my financial backers Max Stolz and Charlie Wittman, without your assistance this project would have been way more difficult.

To my fellow writers in the Non-Fiction Writers Group for their counsel and feedback through the pre-publication process.

To my son, Manuel, for his support, encouragement, and being a sounding board as I developed this book.

To 45+ years of clients ranging from street kids to executives, celebrities, and city mayors who were responsible for forcing me to stay at the top of my game, innovating when there were no stock answers, so that I could best assist them to be at the top of their games and become their best selves.

# Foreword

I recently received a call from a former colleague, Jason Wittman. We worked together in the 1990's in Los Angeles. Other than the occasional humor sharing posts on Facebook, we haven't had much contact. He called, told me that he had finished writing a book and asked would I read it and offer him feedback. In those days, I was the clinical supervisor for programs through an agency that served folks with mental health struggles. We provided support services such as counseling, case management, vocational training, housing, and long-term treatment for co-existing substance problems. Jason was the executive director of a youth program that worked with "street kids" in the Hollywood, CA. I provided some needed Licensed Clinical Social Worker supervision to satisfy a particular grant requirement. You could say I was "moonlighting", literally!

This opportunity gave me the privilege of meeting him at his van (at midnight), stopping off at Starbucks to pick up donated food, and observing his work with the young people who dropped by throughout the early morning hours. He was a safe resource providing ongoing nurturing and guidance. He was also a vital advocate during periods of crisis for these individuals. He was a solid constant in their lives and the true fulfillment of the social work mission to "meet them where they are" when working with clients. Jason even wrote a book about those days called "The Street Shrink Chronicles".

So here we are, each in our late 70's and he asks me to read his new book which he explains was motivated by a comment made by a past mentor - that "doers" don't leave much legacy, no one really remembers what they have done. So, he is writing another book to pass along what he has learned, what has been beneficial to his work, including the bumps along the way.

I too have fond memories of my rewarding career as a social worker: working with severely mentally ill patients in forensic settings (Atascadero State Hospital, Department of Corrections, both within prison and with Oakland Parole Outpatient Clinic. I worked with Jason during my time in the Wilshire District of Los Angeles. But I only reminisce and reflect about those years. Jason wrote this guide to share with all of us. He and I used many of the same techniques in our work, so I thoroughly enjoyed reading this collection of practical approaches to take on some of the most difficult tasks of living a healthy life. It's a combination of his personal journey as well as a guidebook of strategies and tools for dealing with the life problems that most people, especially recovering folks, regularly face.

Jason and I also share a deep appreciation for the 12 step programs. His section on the 12-step is great. I particularly liked the Building Social Graces part, not often identified as a strength of group recovery. I have used Al-Anon 12-step readings and support groups since 1988 for my personal recovery as well as my ongoing work with addicted folks. Jason's book can be read via the philosophy of 12-step: "take what you like and leave the rest". There are so many ideas and paths to follow. Jason leads us toward many paths for self-exploration throughout these pages. I enjoyed reconnecting with an old friend and learning so much more about his own journey as well as refreshing my repertoire of therapeutic strategies and bits of wisdom that he shares here with us all.

I really love this book! It is comprehensive and not a quick read because it captures many thoughts, which I think gives the reader many items to pick as starting points and then can return to expand to the suggestions that didn't immediately click.

Donna Reimann Pedroza, LCSW

# Introduction

While I was a grad student at Cornell University working on my counseling-psychology masters, I was having a conversation with one of my mentors, the late Dr. Urie Bronfenbrenner, who knew how much I hated doing formal research and loved actually starting and running counseling programs. I would regularly wander into his office to describe my latest innovative counseling program or technique. It had already taken me five years to do a two-year master's program because I started and ran one of the first residential therapeutic communities for addicted folks in the country. And then after three years there, I left to develop another first, a counseling program which put master's level counselors out on the streets to outreach teens in their environment, establishing all the rapport necessary for a counseling conversation and having those conversations upon request by the teens.

During one of these impromptu conversations, Dr. Bronfenbrenner stopped me short as I was recounting my latest discovery, with, "There is a problem with you doers! You are going to leave here one day, and no one is going to know what the hell you ever did!" He was right. I had been doing innovative program development from almost the day I stepped back onto the Cornell campus without paying any attention to how others might learn from my efforts.

The result of that conversation was that I finally wrote my thesis, a manual on how to outreach and counsel with street kids, and finally graduated.

What has stayed with me through this long professional journey of mine was Dr. Bronfenbrenner's haunting observation that I would eventually move on and nobody would have a clue as to what I had innovated. I have been writing ever since. This book is the latest of those writings.

## So why this book?

I began my life as a loser. Well, actually, not a loser because no one is a loser, but they just think and act as if they were one. My childhood was a fairly normal one in a very ordinary, loving, and hardworking middle-class home. Even in my earliest recollections of my experiences with other people, I pretty much felt like the odd ball out. Being one of the original 98-pound weaklings at a time when gym class and team sports defined a boy set my thinking up for poor self-esteem. It didn't help that my very loving Mother didn't understand that statements like, "Self-praise stinks!" and "What happened to the other 4 points" (after getting a 96 on a test) were a setup for low self-esteem.

When we were kids, my parents sent my brother and me to summer sleepaway camp in the mountains of Pennsylvania. For the most part, I had a good time, although my most frequent recollection was being teased about having big ears, especially by one fellow camper. Because most of summer camp activities were team ones and I was already not feeling like I could win in that arena, I started on a pattern of coping that lasted through a goodly portion of my early life.

I found activities where I could be the assistant to the adults of the camp. I worked as the assistant to the guy who ran the canteen, became a stable boy and then, as I got older, a junior counselor. All these positions were ones where I could thrive without competing and as a junior counselor, be in charge of those I did not think I could win over as a peer.

In high school, I became the captain of the student monitors (the hall cops), and the student director of the school plays. Although I was not aware of my motivations for being student director,

JASON WITTMAN, MPS, LAADC, CATC-IV

it is quite apparent now that I avoided acting, of which I was terrified. And on and on: in college I was the house manager in a fraternity and the behinds the scene person in student government.

The interesting facet of all of this is that my self-confidence regarding my ability to perform all these activities was ever increasing though I never could, internally, accept the win. By the time I graduated from college, my self-confidence was acceptable enough to become an Air Force officer and lead a multi-million-dollar fuels management organization in Viet Nam, with many personnel under my command. In most of those positions, though, my inner feeling felt like I was a fraud, that somehow, I was able to fool these people into letting me do these things. Today, these feeling would be labeled "Imposter Syndrome" and (spoiler alert) I figured out what the root cause for that is and fixed it, but I am getting ahead of the story.

As you will discover as you journey with me through this book, the only person whose approval ever matters is our own. It took me many years to figure that out. I truly was looking for love and approval in all the wrong places.

It wasn't until I was out of the military and back in Cornell University for a master's in counseling psychology did, I start working on my inner game to increase my self-esteem. Through a somewhat painful process of trial and error, I eventually learned how to like myself.

Once I figured that out, no matter what external stuff was going on, I could still like me, be comfortable being me and even enjoy the challenges. I have done all those things that, in my earlier life, I had avoided. I have competed successfully racing motorcycles, I have acted on stage and on film, even sang in a movie and have been in major leadership positions rather than hiding out as a behind-the-scenes manipulator. Now most of that is due to having developed high self-confidence. The most important part of the process was that I learned how to love me. Once I had achieved that and my insides (the self-esteem) caught up with the great outside accomplishments, there was no longer any imposter syndrome. I was finally able to own my wins without reservation.

Today, I can look my reflection in the mirror and say and totally believe, "Great guy!" I truly love me, as I am. Not only have I walked the walk, but I also have developed the tools to make that walk a lot shorter and less painful for my clients. This is why I am uniquely qualified to guide others through this process of enhancing their self-esteem. Well, this is "why" I do what I do. The "what" and "how" are the "prescriptions' of this book. When followed, these prescriptions work!

If you're curious about my long professional life and some of the interesting, and sometimes off the wall things that I have done in my life, you can go to the "About me" section on my website, http://stage2recovery.com/about-me/

Much of this book is a plan and a prescription of how to happily live within your own skin and then how to walk exquisitely and successfully through and win at the getting on living stuff of life. All of this becomes possible when you learn how to Win at Life. Please read this book as if your life depends on learning the skills I am presenting, because it does!

# SECTION I

## Inner Game Fundamentals

# Prescriptions for Intentionally Creating a Joyous Life

## Living a Balanced Life

*~ All Work and No Play, a Setup for Personal Disaster ~*

### The Work Part~

*The Principle: Any endeavor in life or business can be designed as a winnable game worth playing.*

I fully understand, especially in tough economic times, that sometimes people need to take a job – any job - in order to survive. It is possible to do anything for a limited time, even onerous things, when there is an understanding that there will be an endpoint. But when a job is not one that the individual would choose outside of getting a paycheck; when it's unrewarding, unfulfilling, or both in most cases and this becomes a lifetime of work experience, it can take a toll. No amount of great home life or monetary reward can compensate for the emotional damage of trudging through endless days of unfulfilling work.

The trick that makes life worth living is to find a profession that is both one's pick as a hobby and also lucrative.

Ideally, you want to create a life that has all the elements that will be potentially, if not actually, winnable. AND one where you get to play and do what you love. The degree which you are in a job that is either not winnable or not so enjoyable will create an equal level of dissatisfaction and ill ease.

Many folks, if not most, are living less than ideal lives, even though they are in winnable occupations and doing well. Unfortunately, because they are not in their first choice of a profession they are in great conflict. They are making the money, getting the praise and all the other perks of doing a great job yet in spite all of that, they are less than happy and feel that a part is missing. They are unhappy, unfulfilled, bored. Those whose lives eventually become more complete have figured out that they needed to either change to a more satisfying profession or at least add their dream job into what they are doing.

There's this story of a world-renowned surgeon who really wanted to be a jazz pianist, but he ended up going to med school to satisfy his parents. He became a hugely successful surgeon, renowned in his specialty AND hugely unhappy! He eventually resumed his performing career along with his medical practice and truly lived happily ever after.

Unfortunately, many misread the problem of a mismatch of job and their interests and end up trying to fill the emptiness with all sorts of futile activities and distractions. Some double down, doing more of the same work and becoming workaholics, while others resort to alcohol and/or drugs to cope.

There's also the opposite scenario where some folks are doing exactly what they love but it's not a winning career and they can't provide for themselves and their families. For them, recognizing that what they are doing is a great hobby and searching for an equally satisfying but lucrative career would make it a win-win for them.

Finally, there are those who do not have a clue to any of this and are living a life of quiet desperation, bouncing from one unsatisfying job to another. For these folks, a good career counselor or coach would be a life saver.

The trick to winning at your outer game is to take care of all the stuff of your inner game.

## The Play Part~

*"There is not a shred of evidence that life is supposed to be serious!"*

Having been boss-less most of my life, meaning that I either was an executive running a company or a solopreneur with no one overseeing me, I have learned the hard way that all work and no play is a road that leads to both a lonely existence as family and friends fade away and eventual burn out. Sure, there are times when it is absolutely necessary to do all-nighters to meet a deadline, but when those marathon workdays become a regular occurrence, that is a recipe for disaster in one form or another.

Principle ~ All winnable games worth playing have a beginning, middle and end.

If your work is a winnable game worth playing but if it never ends, then life moves more and more towards unbalanced and increasingly unsatisfying. People who lead balanced lives are able to work as hard as they wish and know that they need to pause every once in a while and stop to smell the roses. They make sure that recreation and family time is part of their daily schedule. In thinking of their work as a winnable game, they keep in mind that that is a daily game that ends at the end of the work period. Just like if they were in a sports game, they evaluate their wins and missteps and plan out the next day's game AND THEN they leave work at work and move on to living their personal lives with equal intensity.

Whether it is at work or at play, remember that life is not supposed to be serious. It is totally possible to bring joy and fun into the work part of life while fulfilling the work mission. Having once had, as Air Force officer the extra duty as mortuary officer, I can report that morticians are only the holy, somber-faced folks you see during funerals when they are interfacing with the public. Behind closed doors in their shop, they carry on and joke like all working folks do, who enjoy their jobs.

JASON WITTMAN, MPS, LAADC, CATC-IV

That is the prescription to living a balanced life and have fun while living it!

## The Dream of Dreams

Just knowing where one's passions are, and what kind of life's work would be most satisfying or fulfilling, is not enough to ensure that in the long run those goals will be achieved. The missing element is what I call, "The Dream of Dreams." The Dream of Dreams is a visualization of what life would look like if one's fondest, most passionate aspirations are happening right now. The Dream of Dreams is like an automatic pilot in an aircraft. The autopilot is an instrument that, once it knows the destination of the plane, will keep the plane on course even when the wind keeps attempting to blow it off course. Autopilots cannot do their work if they do not have specific destinations entered into the system. If an airline pilot was heading to Hawaii from Los Angeles and the pilot gave the autopilot the destination of "West" rather than the exact coordinates of Honolulu Airport, everyone will get very wet when the plane misses the island and runs out of fuel. That is exactly what happened to those folks who did not continually work on their Dream of Dreams.

When the inner mind, which computes visually, gets a clear picture of where the person wants to go, it will automatically keep the person on track. The best way to program the inner mind is through visualization. The following is the visualization process. Please keep in mind that this is something that you should practice, not just a one-time thing. Machines like autopilot in planes only require a one-time setting for them to work. Our inner minds need continual visual suggestions for them to finally get that this is a new program for doing things, a new destination. When it does, they will continue on that course forever. This is why habits are so very hard to get rid of.

All suggestions and imagery must be in the positive, meaning that the inner mind drops the word, "not" out of the suggestion so, "I am not afraid," gets heard as "I am afraid." "I'm feeling very confident," works much better. Because the inner mind only thinks of time as being in the present tense, i.e.: NOW!, with little or no concept of pasts and futures, all imagery must be in the present tense as if it is happening now. It is a strange construction, but the effective form would be, "In 10 years, I AM doing...." not "will be doing ......"

So what is The Dream of Dreams? The Dream of Dreams is that dream that assuming you have all the education you would ever need, all the finances, all the breaks, and all the experience, in other words, every resource you would ever need, would be exactly where you would ultimately like to be ending up in your life. The dream is, incidentally, always under construction. The most important part is that for it to produce the intended results, dreaming it must become a part of one's daily practice.

There was a period in my life when I realized that I was stagnating and not liking what I was doing, workwise. I started depressing myself a bit. Because it was not the me that I am used to. I started an exploration of why this was happening and discovered that because I had actually achieved and had been living my original Dream of Dreams, I had neglected to revise it to include my new goals and life's desires. So my inner mind no longer had a destination and it shut down the creative process; therefore I was in the doldrums.

JASON WITTMAN, MPS, LAADC, CATC-IV

When I take clients through this exercise of forming and imaging The Dream of Dreams, I usually say, "Close your eyes and go inside for a while. Imagine and picture that I have a magic wand and when I tap you on the shoulder, you will be transported to a time in your future when you are in your perfect life. You are doing the things you always most wanted to do and living the life you always wanted to live. You have all the resources and abilities you will ever need to be living the ultimate life. So now picture and imagine that if you were to open your eyes, you would be in that ultimate life. Look around now. What do you see you doing? What is your occupation? Where are you living? Who are your friends and associates? Now look closer and engage all your senses. If you are at work, where are you? If you see yourself as a renowned professor, what does your office look like, what degrees and letters of appreciation are on your wall? What are people telling you and writing about you? If you are a famous actor, picture yourself in the ultimate role in the movies or play of your fondest dreams. What do your surroundings smell like? Who are your co-stars? Notice the rave reviews of your performances hanging on your dressing-room walls. How does that feel? What are you telling yourself about all this success? Picture yourself being interviewed by the TV interviewer who only interviews major celebs. How great does that feel?"

If you have problems drifting off into a nice, relaxed state, I have a progressive relaxation audio program, MP3 that is available, online. As a reader of this book, you can get a free copy download of this program at: https://gumroad.com/l/jjw201/comp1 Regularly listening to the program for about 30 days will link relaxation to your breath and make achieving that state very easy.

If you regularly practice dreaming this Dream of Dreams, always revising it to reflect your current aspirations, it is almost guaranteed that you will someday realize that you are living what you once dreamed of being. That is because your inner mind, once it grabs that this is the destination it is supposed to be moving towards, will automatically get you to make the responsible choices you need to make to keep you on track. The beauty of this technique is that it is a willpowerless solution! Willpower is an outer mind trying to override an inner mind program, an utterly useless effort that usually leads to frustration and failure. Because The Dream of Dreams usually updates that vision directly into your inner mind through visualization, a language it understands, the need to override or try to override its programming is avoided.

One last requirement about visualizing the contents of your dream, it has to be absolutely positive, totally devoid of any downsides or negativity or less than exquisite performance. Job in the Bible, said," What I fear the most is upon me!" I say that what you imagine tends to be realized. If you imagine Doom and Gloom, as Job did, that's what you get! It is okay to include how well you adapt to changing conditions or bits of adversity or how each performance is better than the last. You just have to be vigilant to keep doubts and uncertainties from entering The Dream of Dreams. Remember that the primary assumption for this exercise is that all the prerequisites and conditions are more than favorable to ensure the total success of your The Dream of Dreams.

## Express Your Feelings and Emotions

We as adults tend to withhold the expression of most negative feelings. We withhold what we're really feeling inside and pretending to ourselves and others, oftentimes disastrously, that we're okay. This pattern of keeping our emotions hidden eventually wrecks relationships. It can easily create an internal environment for the growth of addictions and other unwelcomed behaviors, as well as the environment for physical illness. To start with, let's explore why we are set up from an early age to avoid expressing negatives; then I'll describe some of my ideas on how to deal with and express them responsibly.

## How The Boy Code Affects Us All

In order to understand why adults regularly stifle negative feelings, it is useful to go back to explore how that habit was formed and reinforced in early childhood. There is actually a name for this behavior, it is called the Boy Code. The Boy Code is a pervasive, unwritten code that is so ingrained in society that most people, unless they are aware of it, enforce it through their responses and comments to boys from the day they are born.

After working with male teens for many years, I intuitively knew about the boy code and what to do in raising kids to counter it. I am forever indebted, though, to Dr. William S. Pollack for his research on this subject and his great book about raising boys called, " Real Boys: Rescuing Our Sons from the Myths of Boyhood."

This book and others he has written validated my experience and work and gave me a great text and reference guidebook to offer to the parents I coach. Much of the theory I am presenting here is drawn from Dr. Pollack. If every parent who is raising sons would read this early on, their boys would have a far easier time as teens. In "Real Boys" he discusses how the Boy Code influences everything a teen does, how they make decisions and choices, who they date and what feelings they can and cannot express to others. That is just the first chapter; the rest is a fantastic guide for understanding and raising boys.

The Boy Code tells boys and teens (and unfortunately, even grown men) that they must always appear strong by never giving in or showing signs of weakness, being in control of all situations and especially their emotions (except for anger and violence), never admitting to defeat or being wrong, always being macho even when they falling apart inside, being independent by "being a man!" and so on. I am sure that, by now you get the point. The bottom line is that any outward appearance or utterance that might possibly be considered by others as "shameful" is to be avoided. This means that crying when hurt is a no, no. Hanging around mother or girls, except on dates, is to be avoided for fear of being labeled a sissy or the other "f" word, faggot. This is, also why, by the time they become teens, they answer our requests for a conversation about how they are and feel with grunts or two word answers, "I'm O.K.," even when it is obvious that they are not.

Parents who do not understand the Boy Code inadvertently enforce it by their interactions with their boys and set themselves up for many problems with their future teens, including keeping all their feelings inside. In 'Real Boys," Dr. Pollack cites a study that observed parents of newborns. The researchers were watching how the parents interacted with their babies. The results illustrate how the Boy Code messages start being given right out of the womb. The parents of girls mimicked all the facial expressions of their newborn. When she smiled, they smiled. When she frowned, they frowned. The parents of boys only mimicked happy expressions of their baby. When the boy babies frowned or cried, their parents did everything they could including clownish expressions and clowning around to attempt to change their sad moods to happy ones. And we wonder why they won't share their unhappy feelings with us when they are teens!

Besides the obvious, consequences of the Boy Code on teens includes not wanting to share feelings with parents, being obstinate, fighting with siblings, and being bullies.

Other consequences that are of huge concern to society. When they happen, they are blamed on the teens without society taking any of the blame for setting them up. I am referring to youth gang activity including drive-by shootings and to school shootings. Two weeks before the Columbine High School shootings, I

JASON WITTMAN, MPS, LAADC, CATC-IV

heard Dr. Pollack during an interview with Oprah say, "When boys cannot cry, bullets become their tears!" Unfortunately, and prophetically, he was totally right. More unfortunate is that those two boys were totally blamed for all the havoc they created with very little to no culpability laid at the doorstep of our society. The Boy Code of society set up the other students who teased and bullied them, literally to those students' deaths. Society, through the Boy Code, gave the students and faculty permission to tolerate that harassment because "boys will be boys." And, finally, society's Boy Code taught those two kids to hold inside their very hurt feelings until they exploded.

Note, that although the original research was aimed at boys, it bears mentioning that subsequent study has shown that girls, too, have been raised with socially imposed guidelines on what and how to express their feelings.

## Responsible Expression of Feelings

There are only two choices when it comes to feelings; either we express them responsibly or they eventually damage our emotional wellbeing. When repressed feelings are due to unresolved problems with others, they can eventually explode outwardly, as in "I didn't see that coming!" or the straw that broke the camel's back, or inwardly through addictive behavior and ultimately, suicide.

*The hard truth is that there is an imperative for responsible expression.*

In a residential therapeutic community rehab that I ran many years ago, one of the types of groups we ran were called "hostility groups." The rehab was set up with a resident-run structure that paralleled the staff one. There was a built-in pressure-cooker atmosphere when it came to house chores. In the military, they would call that "shit runs downhill!" The overriding rule in the facility was that any negative feelings towards those senior residents or staff must be withheld until a responsibly appropriate time. In the meantime, immediately as the feeling came up, there was blanket permission to go to the "hostility box" and on a form, fill in who was the target of the feelings and the story behind them, sign it, then deposit it in the box and return to work.

Once a week there would be a house hostility group. The staff member running the group would read one of these slips, and then the writer and the target would verbally face off. The only rules for these groups were no physical violence and no one gets out of their seat. There was no regulation as to what was said or how it was expressed (shouting and screaming were quite OK), and both people talking at the same time was also accepted. What ensued was a shouting, screaming, cursing rage-a-thon. Chances were that the accuser was reacting to pressure from the supervisor and the supervisor was receiving corrective pressure from his next level higher up all due to the ineptitude of the worker. This verbal exchange went on until there were these two grinning people facing each other with nothing more to say. Grinning after all that? Yes, and that is the point of this story. On the other side of feelings is blissful release. Not until the two went through this catharsis was the hostility that clouded their thinking and reasoning cleared. At that point, the staff member would calmly talk them through a resolution of the original problem and, more importantly, any therapeutic issues that came out during the verbal battle.

What we were teaching were both the importance of responsibly expressing feelings, including postponing them to an appropriate time, and that ultimately getting those feelings out was essential.

Mark Twain once said that cursing offered a form of relief even denied to prayer. Without getting into a religious discussion, the reason for the relief is more probably from the expression of the feeling than the specific words. For me, there is no debate as to the absolute necessity of expressing feelings, especially negative ones.

The only question remaining is a definition of what responsible expression is. The answer is "it depends."

It depends on many factors: environmental, social, cultural, situational and parental. It might never be responsible to explode verbally and throw things in an office or work situation. The same would apply for parents in the presence of their kids. Some cultures, however, do allow for explosive verbal hostility from bosses and parents. People who grew up in those cultures know, just as in our hostility group, that there would ensue a calm reasonableness after the verbal explosion.

Where such expression is either not tolerated or is too intimidating to others, postponement of the expressions is the rule. I once had a teen foster son who figured out how to do a delayed expression. He would go to the thrift store and buy a dozen dinner plates. When he was particularly agitated, he would take a plate and go out in the alley behind the house and smash it on the sidewalk. He then would calmly have to clean up the mess, which gave him time to process his feelings.

So if the expression of feeling has to be put off, some of the responsible ways to get them out can include physically beating on inanimate objects such as drums, punching bags or even as with my foster son, plates, as long as anyone nearby are pre-warned about the impending explosion. Because they are also able to put you back together after the catharsis, using the services of professional counselors and coaches is most preferable, if they are OK with and can handle full expression. And finally, remembering that we all have a built-in relief valve that has been available from birth to the final departure date, CRYING!! GROWN MEN (AND WOMEN) DO CRY! When I worked crisis lines and had a suicide call, I knew that when I got the caller to cry fully, the chances that they would make it through the night were very high. (I know of at least three babies named after me because their mothers survived the night.)

## The Balancing Act

Yes, I previously addressed this subject. I decided that it is important enough to the quality of one's life that it was worth revisiting it from a slightly different perspective.

Recently in a workshop, I was reminded of the consequences of all work and no play, a rut that people who work for themselves too easily fall into, especially for those of us who work from our homes. Being cognizant of when we are "at work" and when we are "off duty" is very important. People who are always working and putting in double shifts are very likely to become underproductive, which is consistent with the law of diminishing returns. This seems counter-intuitive, especially to this former workaholic, but the truth is that, as the time increases, the effectiveness of the work output and the ability to concentrate diminishes. When this is ongoing, an increasing deficit of sleep and rest will start to affect the quality of output (even early in the day), which will trigger a desire to work even more to cover for it.

Fortunately, we have a built-in mechanism to alert us to when we are getting too obsessed with work. We have an inner personality that yearns for balance. The more work we do in a day, the more our inner being resents the psychic and physical intrusion on its need for the 3Rs: rest, relaxation, and recreation. When the inner being gets resentful of this intrusion, it reacts subtly, or not so subtly, by producing behaviors to get the conscious being to recognize the imbalance.

The moral of this story is to pay attention to the early signs that maybe we are overdoing the work stuff and that our work is way out of balance with the need for the 3Rs. Even better

JASON WITTMAN, MPS, LAADC, CATC-IV

than that is paying attention to the way we plan our days and weeks, as well as life itself, to make sure that there is a healthy mix of hard work and equally strong doses of rest and play. Also, paying attention to getting adequate nutrition completes the prescription for a healthy, happy, and abundant life.

I had a sign over my desk in one of my counseling offices that read "This is not a job; it is a calling!" When people are doing work that fills them with purpose and can hang that sign in their workplace, then they will be working a life worth living. Combining that with playing a life worth living will be truly living a life worth living! We get one life. No rehearsal, no extra chances. If there is a one-sentence dictum to living life fully and happily, it is to ensure that the work we do involves something we are passionate about doing and then be just as passionate about our non-work life.

## Be Like the Mockingbird

I woke up one morning to the sounds of the same mockingbirds that I listened to when I was falling asleep the night before. Actually, I ought to be more specific, it was one mockingbird that was singing its precious little heart out, and who would keep singing until he attracted a mate to mate with. Now this was a bird I could get behind. Loving its life, having a grand old time and playing full out! Talk about 100% enthusiasm and 100% commitment to being fully in the moment!

The late David Goodstein, philanthropist, very successful magazine publisher, and humanitarian prescribed precisely this as the formula for a happy and enjoyable life. He said that no matter what you are doing, do it with 100% enthusiasm and 100% commitment, and it will always be enjoyable. This is an almost stupidly simple yet profound concept.

It was so stupidly simple, in fact, that I couldn't wait until the next time I had sex. Imagine the sublime sex we could have being 100% in the moment of it. I realized that I was never 100% immersed in the action. At least 25% (and many times much more) of me was hovering somewhere up near the ceiling and being very concerned about how well I was performing and what my partner was thinking about my performance. I couldn't wait to apply this concept because I knew that it would greatly improve my enjoyment. As it turned out, I was wrong. It didn't greatly improve my experience; it transformed this heretofore semi-enjoyable, semi-obligatory performance into a mind-blowing experience! It's amazing what results from being totally involved in what one is doing!

I started to apply this concept of being 100% enthusiastic and 100% committed to whatever I was doing at every moment of my life, and it has transformed my experience of my life.

The next time you hear a mockingbird, stop and pay attention. REALLY listen to it. When you are engaged in listening to a child, parent, boss, employee or client, REALLY listen. Bring your whole self into it. Immerse yourself in the experience of listening and nothing else will matter. Not thinking about the lawn that needs mowing. Or what you will have for lunch later. For that matter, when you listen to someone, put your whole self in it. If your mind wonders, remember that the mockingbird is singing for you, someone is talking to you, and for that time, you are fully there with them.

In my years of working as a social worker working with street kids, I had participated in more than my share of heavy drama; racing to emergency rooms with half alive kids, stepping in between hostile kids with guns, and the like. Looking strictly at my personal experience of those events, I thoroughly enjoyed what I was doing, and it was fun. That is not to say that I didn't

JASON WITTMAN, MPS, LAADC, CATC-IV

have heavy emotions about what was going on. I did, but usually after the action was over. Because I was 100% into doing what I was doing as I was doing it with total commitment and enthusiasm, I was having great fun and enjoyment, and I was at the top of my game.

When I am with a client, I am fully present in the dialogue. My 100% commitment, enthusiasm and attention is in the moment with the birdsong or with my client. No matter what the content of that dialogue, it is always fun and a hugely enjoyable experience. Playing full-out with 100% enthusiasm and 100% commitment is how one gets to the top of one's game. Being at the top of one's game as it is being played full-out with 100% commitment and 100% enthusiasm is always fun!

## Coming from Effect Vs Coming for Cause

I was introduced to the concept of effect vs cause by Dr. Michael Durst, author of a great book, "Napkin Notes on the Art of Living" (available on Amazon.com). Once the concept is learned, it becomes really clear how to create winning experiences in one's life.

There are two ways of viewing one's experience of life. The first is from the perspective of effect. When the world is viewed as "coming from effect" or "assuming the position of effect", your experiences of life are seen as being the effect of what people, places and things do to or for you. You are either looking for a savior or being the victims and blaming your current wretched state of lousy outcomes on everyone and everything other than yourself.

Statements that start with, "If it only....," or "if they only..." are effect statements. They are declaring that life would be much better if something or someone other than you would produce the miracle. Blaming lousy experiences on others are also effect statements. Country songs and blues would be lost without effect statements, such as, "She stole my heart and stomped that sucker flat!" As if anyone truly has that ability to actually do that to a partner who is powerless to stop it. My father understood this concept because anytime someone uttered an iffy statement, he would respond with, "and if I had four wheels, I would be a trolley car!" Coming from effect is a celebration of victimhood and endarkenment.

The other, and more useful way of viewing their experience of life is "from cause." When assuming the position of "cause," we understand that we are cause of ALL our experience of life. Notice I said "we are cause," not we are THE cause." There are many reasons why you have the experiences you have that might be beyond your control. If we are coming from Cause, we will recognize that regardless of why something is the way it is, if we do not like that something, we have 100% responsibility for making the necessary adjustments to change our experience to a more palatable one.

Viewing life this way gives you the ability to be master of your experiences because you take full responsibility for yourself in life. When you think this way you understand that if you do not like your experience of life, you need to do something different. You can make changes in the situation, leave or bail out, or choose to stay and ride it out knowing that it is your choice to do so. There is an old saying, "If you always do what you always did, you'll always get what you always got. If you want something different, you have to do something different." After you recognize that you are cause of all your experience of life, hopelessness, victimhood and endarkenment disappear.

When I was an undergraduate at Cornell University, I had a professor who would be my nominee for the "Coming from Cause" award if there was one. The late Professor Dan Sisler was, in his earlier life, a very athletic young man. He joined the Air

Force after college and became a survival specialist who taught pilots how to survive in very cold weather.

But an accident left him totally blind. If he had been a person who viewed his experience as coming form effect, he would have most probably blamed everything and everyone for his accident and then expected the military, the Veterans Administration and the world to provide for his every need. Not Dan. When he was confronted with a setback or problem, he had an "OK, now what do I do to rise above this?" attitude. He was one of the most self-sufficient people I have ever met.

Here are a few exemplary notes from his life after blindness:

He lived out in the country within walking distance of his office at the University. He walked with a cane, to and from his office every day, even in the winter snows. He once told us why he didn't have a seeing eye dog. He said that after he was able to navigate the country roads and the tangle of sidewalks and quads on the way to his office and then being able to find his office in a huge office building, he didn't want to have to pat a dog on the head and thank him for getting him there safely. Rather he preferred to pat himself on the back and say, "Dan, you old rascal, you've done it again!" Also, as a professor of economics and marketing, he lectured from braille notes and used the blackboard like a sighted person, writing charts and graphs and paragraphs of text to illustrate his lectures. By the way, he continued to downhill ski, with someone to act as his eyes.

Here is an example of this principle. This story has two different possible endings depending on the guy's way of dealing with the experience:

**Facts:** A guy is about to cross a street. He does everything he can possibly do to make sure that it is safe to cross the street. Halfway across that street, a drunk driver races around the corner and nails him. He loses his legs and is in a wheelchair for the rest of his life.

**The rest of the story "coming from effect":** For the rest of his life, he blames that driver for changing his life so drastically and looks for everyone, but himself to make his life better. He feels that the State owes him a livelihood because "there ought to have been a light on the corner," and the insurance company ought to have given him more money. Poor me, Poor me......

**The rest of the story "coming from cause":** He knows that the drunk has 100% responsibility for hitting him, and he has 100% responsibility for being there. What is more important is that he knows that he has 100% responsibility for his experiences in life now and in the future, so he says to himself, " O.K. now what do I do to create a great life with what I've got?" He then embarks on a new journey with the new givens in his life (no functioning legs), playing this new game with its new rules totally full-out, just as he did with the old rules before the accident. Some real-life examples of this are the publisher Larry Flint who, after losing the use of his legs, continued to function 100% and built a publishing empire. Another is the great psychiatrist, hypnotherapist and teacher, Milton Erickson, MD, who refused to become a "victim" of polio and worked with the hand he was dealt and created the great life he had.

In relationships, to give another example of those coming from effect will feature battling partners, constantly blaming each other for perceived troubles, will see themselves as victims, and, if asked, will propose that the cure of the problem is for the partner to do things differently. When people come from cause, the question becomes, "what can I do differently to improve the situation" or, if the situation becomes untenable, they will work on quickly removing themselves.

> After a lifetime of "coming from effect" thinking, it is important to constantly monitor our self-talk to make sure that it is staying in the "how can I change my experience of life" rather than expecting other people, places, and things to do something to or for me to change my experiences. When we notice we are using "if statements" an immediate response should be to change the phrase to a "cause statement" as in "what can I DO" rather than "if it only could..." .

## A Better Way to Label the Feeling of Shutting Down (formerly known as depression)

I learned this concept from one of my mentors, the late William Glasser, MD., author of many books including "Reality Therapy", "Positive Addiction" and "Choice Theory." He taught that by labeling this set of feelings with the noun, "depression," and then describing it via the metaphor of a fog, i.e., "*it* descends upon me and I can't do much while I am in *it* and I have to wait until *it* lifts" renders the person a helpless victim because it assigns the cause and the ability to do something about it, to something external to one's self.

He suggested that changing the word "depression" to its verb form, "depressing" gives a path to a remedy." "Depressing" is a negative action verb akin to vegetating. The remedy to a negative action is a positive one. If I am shutting down and depressing, the remedy is to get moving, get into action, to uplift.

When I start to notice that I am depressing myself, I quickly get into action, doing at least little things that will show a positive result. If nothing else, I start cleaning. Straightening a desk or cleaning a sink produces an immediate sense of accomplishment, albeit a small one.

Once I have gotten into action and the desire to depress myself subsides, I can then explore what brought on the feelings of wanting to shut down and can tackle that cause to prevent future shutdown feelings. A little precaution though: not doing this last step of exploring the root causes and just staying busy can easily lead to becoming a workaholic.

# Prescriptions for Creating an Inner Self that Works

## Self-Esteem/Love and Self-Confidence ~ two very different concepts

### Self-esteem and self-confidence are not the same

Although the terms self-esteem and self-confidence are usually associated with each other and sometimes used synonymously or interchangeably, they are not the same. They have different meanings and functions.

Self-esteem is a measure of one's feelings of self-love and self-worth,
whereas
Self-confidence is a measure of one's evaluation of one's ability to perform a task or a skill.

Self-esteem develops from experiences and situations that have shaped how you view yourself today. It is how you feel about yourself overall. To have healthy self-esteem is to have a positive regard for yourself, to truly love yourself.

Self-confidence is how you feel about your abilities, how well you can do things. This varies from situation to situation.

These two are very different and operate independently although there can be serious emotional problems when there is a mismatch between one's internal evaluation and external performance.

## Symptoms of Low/No Self-Esteem or When These are Present, Self-Esteem Isn't

### The Imposter Syndrome

Although it is quite possible to develop a great degree of self-confidence without an equally high self-esteem, it is certainly a less than optimal state to be in. In the case of high performing individuals such as rock stars and high-power executives, oftentimes their self-esteem has not caught up with the hugely increased self-confidence fueled by their meteoritic rise to fame and fortune. The dichotomy between high-flying outsides (confidence) and the insides (esteem) that cannot recognize their innate abilities and accept well-deserved accolades is called The Imposter Syndrome.

When a person's performance greatly overshadows their level of self-esteem, they are susceptible to feeling like a fraud. The accompanying internal dialog (self-talk) is along the lines of *"if they only knew how much I'm messing up"* or *"when they discover the real me, I'm toast!"* That paranoia of being "found out" can be enough to trigger a variety of coping behaviors including addictions, paranoia, suicide, and perfectionism.

What Imposter Syndrome is not: From lots of comments in groups devoted to this subject, many people mislabel their inability to do things because they do not think they can, as Imposter Syndrome. One becomes an Imposter when they actually perform exquisitely and discount the reality of that performance. If one feels that they can't perform and give up attempting to so, that is a self-confidence issue, pure and simple and can be overcome using the tools for building self-confidence. By labeling a self-confidence issue as Imposter Syndrome is clocking it with an emotional misdirection that doesn't allow for the tools to build self-confidence to be used.

>>> The Imposter Syndrome vanishes when one's self-worth, esteem, and love are enhanced to the point where they can finally accept ownership for achievements and talents.

## Perfectionism

Perfectionists are an interesting group. They have little or no self-esteem and are usually fairly high performers in what they do. Their paranoia of being judged as less than perfect leads them to attempt to do everything perfectly. Unfortunately, perfection is impossible to attain, so they continually fail to reach their self-set goals, which creates a feedback loop that reinforces their negative self-evaluations and totally feeds into the feeling of being an imposter and a charter member of the Imposter Syndrome society. That, in turn, feeds into the obsession and another addiction is born.

Most people with low self-esteem including, unfortunately, many people in recovery, also have a similar feedback pattern. Less obvious, it appears as a habit of harsh self-criticism of their actions, their appearance, and just about anything else that touches their lives. Unlike the perfectionist, they are not obsessed with rectifying their uncovered flaws. They use their harsh self-criticisms and both actual and imagined failures as proof of their negative self-evaluations. These folks rarely give themselves an even break. For them, the cup is always half empty. They beat themselves up at the drop of a hat. The slightest criticism from a boss, peer, or even a client can throw them into a depressive state akin to giving up.

High school age underachievers are a good example of this. Although usually misdiagnosed as kids lacking motivation, they are very smart but with very low self-esteem. Actually, they have very high motivation. It takes considerable motivation for a smart kid to intentionally fail. These are young folks who think of themselves as potential failures (aka, losers) and who voluntarily take themselves out of the competition. That way they don't risk being actual failures and have a perfect cover story, "I could have won, but I chose not to play." They are perfect candidates for a variety of addictions.

## Narcissism

Like all these symptoms (all of the addictions) of low to no self-esteem/love, that are misunderstood by the mental health professions and given their own billing in the catalog of mental "diseases," narcissism is nothing more or less than a disparate attempt to counter that empty hole inside, that feeling of worthlessness, by both creating and broadcasting personal fiction about one's greatness and an incessant need for others to offer praise and validation. In the 12 Step programs, they refer to this as rampant ego that needs to be quashed. They are on the right track but, because they are misunderstanding the root cause are prescribing the wrong remedy. Rather than quashing anything, working on building a healthy self-esteem/love from within will cure both the runaway ego problem and its ultimate manifestation, narcissism.

## The Law of Opposites

I have a simple way of understanding just how people are feeling inside. I call it the Law of Opposites. Whatever people have to incessantly tell you about themselves; you can bet that they are feeling the opposite on the inside. Bullies, both physical and verbal, are actually wimps on the inside who are employing" the best defense is a good offence" weapon that keeps their victims far enough away to not be able to see their flaws. Shakespeare understood this law when he had Queen Gertrude in "Hamlet" say, in response to the Player Queen's continual declarations, *"The lady doth protest too much, methinks"* implying that she doesn't really mean what she says.

## Little or no self-esteem is the root cause of all addictions and most other mental maladies.

**Why it is The Root Cause:** I have always had a problem with the medical model that a physical allergy or disease is the root cause of alcoholism and chemical addictions. It does not explain the cause of chemical type addictions (including alcohol) and it absolutely doesn't explain non-chemical ones like food addictions, narcissism, compulsive gambling, and compulsive sex. I have observed many recovering folks who, with numerous years clean and sober, pick up non-chemical addictions. If the allergy explanation was the whole story, then working the 12 Steps for one of the chemical addictions should cover all the addictions, but it doesn't. The same thing is true for a spiritual malady allegedly being the root cause. Working a great spiritual program also doesn't seem to protect against switching addictions. Something is missing...

A clue to the real root cause of all addictions can be found by carefully listening in on meetings of 12 Step programs, regardless of the addiction, to members sharing their "how it was" stories. Somewhere in those shares, they will usually state how, when they took that first drink, hit, sex act, gambling game win or whatever, it filled *"that empty hole inside of me!"* The story is approximately the same across all addictions, be they chemical or non-chemically ones. The narrative usually continues with a rendition of feelings of wellbeing and relief, along with a new ability to do many things that heretofore they were inhibited from doing.

Everyone talks about *"filling that empty hole,"* but few bother to ponder what exactly that hole represents and more important, what was not present that cause that hole in the first place. As best as I can figure out, that missing ingredient is self-esteem/love. Occasionally, a lack of self-confidence, too, can be a cause, but always low or no self-esteem/love.

I had a client who, when describing his feelings when he attended his first AA meeting, said, "The speaker was talking about how when he was newly recovering, he had very low self-esteem. I thought to myself, 'God, I wish I was able to have very low self-esteem! Right now, I have none!'"

We are about to do a deep dive into how to build great Self-Esteem/Love. When people love themself unconditionally and totally, "that empty hole" is filled and the need for any addictive behavior will disappear! This is the best relapse prevention!

## Learning Self-Enhancing Techniques to Boost Self-esteem

If lack of self-esteem is the core problem that drives people to adopt maladaptive behaviors (addictions) in a futile attempt to cover up or mask the hurt caused by "that empty hole inside," it stands to reason that once folks have developed great self-esteem and self-love, the empty hole will be truly and permanently filled. With no empty hole, the need for any addictions, chemical or otherwise, will be over.

For this reason, to achieve full and permanent recovery, a major component of treatment needs to be teaching the tools that effectively promote positive self-esteem. Many of these tools are quite simply taught and, through daily repetition; are quite effective. There usually will be noticeable improvement in the degree of self-esteem after as little as a month of daily practice.

It should be emphasized that an important part of the process of developing high self-esteem/love is the working of the 12 Steps, especially through Step 9. Steps 3 - 9 will go a long way in dealing with old accumulated negative feelings. It is very difficult to work on self-esteem when "the real self" is viewed through lenses clouded by accumulated negative feelings that working The Steps will alleviate. As those negative feelings are eliminated, space opens up for self-esteem to grow and, with these new self-enhancing habits firmly in place, that new self-esteem will grow automatically and exponentially!

## My Prescriptions for Building Self-Esteem

Although building and enhancing one's self-esteem is a lifelong project, there are many techniques that will jump-start that process and assist in continuing that quest to like oneself. Here are seven of my favorites. The first one, the Mirror Exercise, being the best and most essential.

### The Mirror Exercise

This is one of the most powerful techniques to build self-esteem. I have been practicing this technique for many years, and it has been the most important tool to my developing a high level of self-esteem. Its simplicity belies its power. Just do it as I present it and you will be pleasantly surprised by its effectiveness. My clients who have adopted this practice all report similarly great results!

This exercise accomplishes a couple of things. It very effectively builds self-esteem and, because repeatedly smiling upon seeing one's face will make the face become a trigger to a smile, it becomes an automatic recovery tool for when you are in a down-state or a funk. It is impossible to feel bad and smile at the same time, so that smile will break that down-state, giving you an opportunity to move to a better state. Also, the continual recitation of verifiably nice things about yourself, gives your inner mind the repetition it needs to update its pictures of your true worth.

The Mirror Exercise:
   From now on, every time you see your reflection in a mirror, you must:

1. Smile even if you don't want to. Fake a smile if necessary.
2. Say one verifiably nice thing about yourself. That nice thing must be something that you 100% believe is true. That nice thing can't be an affirmation (which is basically a lie that you tell yourself enough time until your inner mind believes it is true.) It must be one that you know, without a doubt is true about yourself. It can be something external, such as your great looks (if you really believe, 100% that they are great) or, preferably, an internal quality such as you're being a loving person, highly intelligent, etc.
      One caveat though...
3. If you use the mirror to beat yourself up, you must come up with two nice things for every nasty one! Most people's worst habit is beating themselves up and the best way of replacing a habit is doing another one more, hence rule #3.

## Take the Win

There are opportunities to reinforce self-esteem that are regularly missed. What is even worse is that those opportunities are converted into reinforcers of lousy self-feelings due to inappropriate responses. For people who are in the habit of putting themselves down, their usual responses when given a compliment is to negate it. For example, when complimented on the beautiful tie or other pieces of apparel, they have to tell how they got it on sale or at a thrift shop, or when thanked for providing some special service, respond with "Oh, it was nothing."

The only appropriate answer to compliments is, "Thank you!" They are not complimenting the manufacturer of that clothing; the compliment is your tastes and your choices of clothing. To take the win, just acknowledge it with a "Thanks." The same goes for compliments about things you do or did. Just say "thank you." That makes the complement yours.

**Compare and Despair Rabbit Hole**

One of the easiest ways to beat yourself up is to compare your insides with someone else's outsides. It is a good example of the follies of attempting mindreading. The reason this is a disastrous endeavor is that what you observe about other people is what they want you to see. It does not necessarily match the way they feel. Assuming that their appearance or the things they own or tell you they are doing reflect their feelings about themselves or their feelings about all those goodies, accomplishments, or, most important, themselves is pure folly. All you know is what you observe. You do not know any of the back stories. That apparently very successful entrepreneur might be upside down in debt attempting to keep that enterprise afloat and be on the verge of suicide though he appears to be happy, successful, and content. To then compare that assumption with your own feelings is a great way to instantly feel bad and less than.

If you understand the law of opposites, this folly becomes even more apparent. The law of opposites is that what people must keep telling you or showing you about themselves is most probably the opposite of the way they feel about themselves. The bully keeps people far enough away, so they never get even a glimpse of their internalized failings. The aggressive, brave face of the bully, the overly tattooed tough-guy appearance and the ostentatious show of jewelry and expensive looking watches, are usually skin-deep and serve their purpose well if you get mislead by them.

I call this a rabbit hole because the more you try to evaluate your being by comparing you with other folks' outsides, the more you will come out feeling like a loser and sink into that pit of despair. Winners only compare themselves today with themselves yesterday or some period ago and revel in the improvement.

### Psycho-semantics

Psycho-semantics are words that have a very different emotional or meta-message (the underlying message) than their dictionary definition. Emotionally they carry way more weight than one would think.

*Try* – The first and most important of these words is "try." Although "try" is used with the general understanding that it is an attempt that will be carried through to completion, its meta-message is that the inner mind already knows that there will be little action attached to the attempt. The chance of success or even starting is very low.

When you hear yourself saying that you will "try" to do something, your inner mind is already discounting any chance of successful completion of the task. This one will be dead on arrival. When your friend tells you he will try to call you, don't hold your breath. It is not going to happen. If he really wanted to call you, he would have said, "I will call you on Tuesday of next week.

I have banished "try" from my vocabulary when used as a synonym for "attempt." It is OK to "try" on a new pair of shoes, but to "try" to clean my desk is a sign to me that I already know the negative outcome.

*Should vs. Could* – "Should" carries lots of emotional weight. Regardless of whether it is used as self-talk or by others about a suggested course of action for you, its meta-message is that if you do not do what is suggested, you are a bad person and ought to be ashamed. If you are already full of shame, "shoulds" can be counted on to reinforce those negative feelings.

The better choice is "could," because "could" has little or no emotional weight. It just suggests a choice, do it or not, it's just a choice. If it doesn't work out, there is no blame or shame. If doing it is important enough, you will do it, or else just make another choice.

*Must or Have to vs. Could or Choose to* – These fall into the same area as "should." The meta (underlying) message is that not only do you have no choice, but if you do not do it or fail to achieve having done it, you are a bad person. Using "could" or saying, "I choose to" takes the emotional weight off of the thought.

**Positive Self-Talk**

Most people with low self-esteem are in the habit of putting themselves down. This is the habit of habits, and there is a whole section of this book devoted to overcoming it. Suffice to say, negative self-talk is one of the most effective ways of maintaining a negative opinion of oneself. Some examples of negative self-talk include:

**Mislabeling positive experiences and accomplishments**

I remember listening to a person sharing about a perfectly chaotic day he just had. He labeled himself as, "I was so crazy today!" and then went on to describe all the crazy things that happened and the difficult people and situations he had perfectly handled and through which he had exquisitely navigated. Instead of labeling the day as a crazy one, he called himself crazy. By mislabeling his skillful performance, he missed an opportunity to give himself some good compliments and take the win.

**Using negative outcomes and poor choices to beat up oneself**

Have you ever said to yourself, "How stupid was I (or that)!" or "God, am I dumb!" or something similar? These are self-putdowns that reinforce loser feelings. The truth is that we learn through trial and error. Winners understand that what is labeled as failure is in fact just feedback. Pure and simple, it just didn't work. No blame or shame, just a learning experience so that by better crafting the next attempt, there could possibly have a better outcome.

**Dismissing and down-playing compliments**

This was covered in detail in the "Take the Win!" section above.

Eliminating all negative self-talk will go a long way towards building a great self-image, especially if it is replaced with positive self-talk by giving oneself mini-compliments, maxi-compliments using the mirror exercise, and making sure to always take the win by merely saying, "thank you!"

Many of us were raised with the idea that self-praise indicates a lack of humility. My mother used to say, "Self-praise stinks!" anytime we gave ourselves credit or compliments. What a terrible thing to teach a kid! That robs a person of the basic tool for building self-esteem. If I am prohibited from recognizing my worth, I am beholden on others to tell me I'm OK. If the only way to get those good feelings is when others tell me or throw bits of praise, there is little opportunity to build internal self-love/esteem and is a perfect setup for codependency.

Religion preaches humility, and 12-Step programs talk about busting/smashing the ego. Both of those concepts are misinterpreted as a prohibition for self-praise. Those concepts are about bragging about one's abilities and obsessively needing to "one-up" everyone, which are activities that people with low or no self-esteem engage in to cover up how bad they feel about themselves. That is very different from being able to recognize and accept one's positive values, achievements, and accomplishments in a way that does not put down or trample on others.

There is an ancient Buddhist saying that *"If you meet the Buddha on the road, kill him!"* What is meant is that the Buddha, being an enlightened soul, has achieved total self-love and acceptance, and has no need for any recognition or praise from others. If you met the real Buddha on the road, you would not know he was the Buddha because he has no need to tell you. Therefore, if you meet someone on the road who tells you he is the Buddha, he must be an imposter.

People with high self-esteem and self-love have little or no need for external recognition of their essence, therefore they can be understated in their dealings with others. Of course, praise and compliments from others are nice, but not necessary. "The ego" that 12-Step programs refer to when they say there is a need to "smash the ego" is actually the bravado and braggery that are poor attempts to cover up and compensate for low self-esteem. That is what drives bullies to be bullies. The way to smash that ego and to be humble is to build up a strong, positive evaluation of one's self. Humility is not subjugating oneself to others, but rather being comfortable enough in one's skin to have the luxury of being able to support others in their journey towards self-love.

### The STOP! Technique

There's a wonderful technique for effectively interrupting negative self-talk and getting you back on a positive track. As with most techniques and methods I write about, this is one I use for myself. Before I describe the "Stop Technique," itself, I need to set the stage, so to speak, by explaining what is going on in the mind when negative self-talk is incessantly occurring.

Although I am sure that brain scientists would not be able to find in their research what I am about to describe, I find this is a useful way to explain what is going on in our minds when negative thoughts abound. The mind operates like a committee of parts (or voices.) Each part has specific tasks that it is responsible for. Some of the prime players are the creative part, that invents new ways of doing things, and the protective part, that wants to make sure that the person will remain OK and will do whatever it thinks is necessary to protect the being to keep it safe. It is this latter one that sometimes, in an effort to ensure that we remain OK, will go to extremes. I view all the parts as benevolent in that they are doing what they do because they think they are acting in our best self-interests. Sometimes though, the methods they adopt and utilize to achieve their goals are lousy ones.

For instance, the part that keeps folks smoking cigarettes actually has good intentions. It wants the smoker to be at ease while being alert as well as giving him something to do with his hands in uncomfortable social situations. Cigarettes do all those things but, unfortunately, the smoker gets slowly destroyed in the process. Good intention – lousy choice of method.

The same is true for that part that keeps generating negative self-talk and paranoid thoughts. Its good intention is to protect the person against doing or thinking anything that might lead to failure or disappointment. It's a lousy method though because it causes inaction or over-cautiousness which can produce that ultimate failure that it wanted to prevent.

When I become aware that that part of the mind is engaged in incessant negative self-talk or conjuring up doomsday scenarios about current activities, potential partners or current projects, I engage the three-part "Stop Technique."

So here is the "Stop Technique": The first thing I do is, either out loud or to myself if there are others present, to say, forcefully, "STOP!" I say it in the same voice as if I wanted to command a child who keeps nagging and nagging me to do something for him to the point that I am ready to do grave bodily damage, to shut up. As I say "STOP!" I take my hand, palm forward and push it out and down (towards the little demon). I say and do this with enough force and positive intention that it will get the child, or in our case, the mind, to stop making noise at least for the moment.

Step two is to use this period of silence to take a deep breath and go inside and talk to that part of the mind that is generating the negativity. Acknowledge and thank it for its good intention and let it know that you received and considered its messages. Then invite the part to quietly observe how your new ways of doing things are working out, letting it know that it could always, in the future, point out impending problems, but that, at this point, just observing without comment would be appreciated.

The third step in this process is to say to yourself, "Now, where was I?" which will bring you and your attention back to whatever footwork you were doing before the negative thoughts or voices interrupted that process.

This may work for you the first time through. The chances are, though, that it might take repeated efforts before the inner mind understands that you will no longer be sidetracked by negative thought.

## Doing Esteemable Acts

This is one of those long recognized "good things" to do. In the Jewish religion, these acts are called *mitzvahs*. They define a mitzvah as an act or deed that deserves a blessing. Mitzvahs are framed as things done to please God. More practically, these are acts that generate internal good feelings and greatly contribute to enhancing self-esteem.

There are two types of esteemable acts, ones the recipient know about and ones done anonymously. Although both are worth doing, the second type, the anonymous ones, seem to benefit the doer's self-esteem the most. Most likely that is because they are totally without any chance of recognition or secondary gain from the recipient, so they are an absolutely pure good deed.

## Change to a More Esteemable Physical Appearance

I need to preface this with the disclaimer that these suggestions are strictly inner-focused. The only consideration that is important in deciding to adopt the suggestions is how they will affect your internal evaluation of yourself.

Physical appearance has a lot to do with how we feel about ourselves. On a purely physiological level, how our clothing fits can directly affect our level of comfortability. An old Chinese proverb by the philosopher Chuang Tzu states, *"If the shoe fits, the foot forgotten, when the belt fits, the belly is forgotten, when the heart is right, 'for' and 'against' are forgotten."* That means the only time we are aware of our feet is when there is a degree of discomfort caused by ill-fitting shoes. Likewise, with your belly. Is your being overweight and your ill-fitting clothes a cause of physical discomfort? If so, make the changes needed to eliminate those discomforts. Doing it just to win the approval of others could have negative hit on your self-esteem. If your heart is right, that you unconditionally love yourself, then other people's judgement or perceived judgements of you are of no concern to you.

Now look in the mirror. Do you like what you see? Would you feel better about yourself if you were wearing a different style? What about your hairstyle"? Does it represent the way you would like to feel about yourself? Are you comfortable with your weight? These questions are designed to let you evaluate the relationship between your appearance and your self-acceptance. I attempted to ask the questions in a way that there would be no assumed value in the answer. The bottom line here is that both our physical appearance and our choices of clothing and style play a very important role is our acceptance and love for ourselves.

I have had mixed feelings in writing this section because I know that a lot of our usual choices and evaluations of our appearance is driven by our buying into the norms of our environment. In a business environment where the norm is tie and jacket, one might feel mighty less-than, showing up in vacation clothes. Dressing appropriately for the environment, though, is the bare minimum. Let's say that a tie and jacket are the prescribed dress. The point of this section is that wearing ill-fitting, wrinkled, and poorly color-matched tie, jacket and slacks will be a very different feel than a well-tailored, smart, well-fitting outfit. Both are societally acceptable, though only the latter promotes internal good feelings.

A book published in 1975 was titled "Dress for Success." Although the main thrust of that book is about dressing to influence others, I believe that what is really going on with those that follow the books dictates is that dressing in clothes that make them feel good adds to self-esteem. This, in turn, automatically translates into the projection of certainty and confidence necessary for successful interactions with others.

It is time to take a physical inventory of yourself. This inventory is to evaluate how you feel about your current appearance. Is your current appearance supporting good feelings about yourself? If it isn't, then you just might take the steps to remedy that mismatch.

One last thought on physical appearance. All of the above really has to do with the topping on the cake. This is self-esteem building 201. The main focus has to be on the cake, of being able to look yourself in the eye and see yourself stark naked in the mirror and be able to like you, <u>AS IS.</u> If nothing else ever changed, if you never lost or gained another pound, to be able to say to yourself in the mirror, "I really love and accept you, as is!" and mean it. With that solid foundation (the cake), the appearance enhancement stuff just adds to the good feelings. Without that solid foundation, all this outside stuff can easily become just another addiction. I used to have a gymaholic, bodybuilder client with a body most would kill for who never felt he had enough muscle because he was building muscle on top of an "I don't like me" foundation.

### Use Self-Hypnosis programs to Reprogram a Positive Self-Concept

Self-hypnosis programs have assisted me and many of my clients to speed up the process of self-acceptance. There has always been some criticism and mysticism surrounding hypnosis. It is totally unwarranted. Plain and simple, all hypnosis is, is allowing our outer mind (the conscious) to drift off into a pleasant trance state so that the inner mind, where all of our programming hangs out can become available for suggestions to change. Normally, the outer mind's main function is to guard the inner mind against change, so consciously attempting to change inner thought is a long tedious process of constant repetition of the new behavior or thought until the inner mind finally accepts it as the new operating program. Hypnosis and self-hypnosis MP3 programs are very effective tools to reprogram the inner mind directly and quickly.

I have produced and marketed such MP3 programs for not only enhancing self-esteem, but also increasing self-confidence, improving the inner game of salesmanship, and maximizing physical potential. I used them myself, so I know they work. You can read all about them and how they work on my self-hypnosis program website: http://innergametools.com/

## The Habit of Habits, Beating Oneself Up and How to Overcome It

*NOTE:* Later, when I describe how to do Steps 6-7 of the 12 Steps, we get to work on eliminating character defects, most of which are bad habits, but for now, let's expose the worst of those habits and suggest how to deal with it.

I start with the assumption that the root cause of all addictions is the lack of self-esteem. The Habit of Habits, thinking and acting like a loser, serves to perpetuate and reinforce those feelings of little or no self-esteem. In my hunt for the root cause of all addictions, I found that listening to recovery stories also provided many clues regarding the Habit of Habits. Besides the theme of "that empty hole inside" the other recurring theme is descriptions of having felt or still feeling "less than" one's peers, and for many, feeling "less than" from early childhood.

Notice that I say "thinking and acting like a loser", without describing people as losers. People are not losers. They just have gotten in the worst of all habits of thinking and acting as if they were. Why? Because their life's experiences have failed to give them the tools for building self-esteem, so that, over time, they start thinking of themselves as "less than' those who have what they admire.

As we already discussed in the last section, this Habit of Habits also drives the underachievers, the bullies, and the narcissists. So how do people reinforce this habit of habits, i.e. thinking and acting like a loser? Perfectionism or beating oneself up at the drop of a hat, not giving oneself the benefit of the doubt and misinterpreting rejection are three major ones.

**Perfectionism** is the ultimate example of loser thinking and acting. Because perfection is an unreachable goal, perfectionists judge their performance against perfection and always come up short. This supplies them with a continual source of negativity. The only thing perfectionists do perfectly is to beat themselves up!

**Not giving oneself the benefit of the doubt:** This is a close cousin to the perfectionist though to a lesser degree and with less obsessiveness. We miss opportunity to quickly recover from situations that didn't turn out to our liking when those events are used as a reason to say negative things about ourselves by making one-time events into universal generalizations. For example, "Can't you ever get this right?" "That was a pretty stupid mistake/You really are a dumb sh*t!" These folks have no recognition that the road to greatness is pathed with errors. That it is the learning process. Michael Jordan missed close to 50% of his shots and still was the best ever!

**Rejection, or the not-so gentle art of mindreading:** Mindreading is when you think that someone else is thinking something that they think they are not thinking at all! When folks have a poor concept of themselves, they automatically misinterpret interactions with other people as something wrong within themselves. A great example of this is in dating, where a negative response to a proposal is automatically interpreted as a rejection. The same can happen in business situations.

It might actually be true that the "no" from the date or business associate was based on a negative evaluation of the person making the proposal. However, the only information available to the proposer at the moment of the "no" response is that, at that moment in time, the decision was made to not participate. There is zero other information that would lead to taking that "no" as a rejection. Thus, that, or any other conclusion, is pure speculation and mindreading. All the proposer knows is that, at that time, place, and moment, for reasons unknown, the other person chose not to participate.

The feeling of rejection comes from bad self-feelings that automatically assume that the rejection is based on a negative evaluation of you. Think of times that you said no to someone's proposal that had totally to do with your own situation, an "ex" just walked in the room, you were too tired, bloated, gaseous, etc. and prayed that you would get another opportunity to then say yes.

How to deal with the feelings of rejection: It's been said that in sales, the average number of no's before a yes is nine! The first no has too little information to accurately evaluate intention, so if it's important, follow up. Leave the offer open with a "perhaps another time?" type of response and if you are really interested, make some other attempts at another time.

The short answer for dealing with feelings of rejection, in a dating situation, for instance having asked someone to dance, is, as you are walking away, mutter to yourself under your breath and out of earshot, "Babes, you do not know what you just missed!" Embrace the truth of that statement and ask someone else!

## Breaking Any Habit – a bit of theory

Before I explain how to break the Habit of Habits, here's a little bit of theory on how to break any habit. It is important to understand; habits are controlled by the inner mind (which is sometimes referred to as the subconscious or unconscious mind). Once the inner mind understands that an action or way of thinking or behaving is normal and natural, it will automatically continue to do it forever. Willpower is a function of the outer mind (sometimes called the conscious mind). The reason willpower hardly ever works to overcome set habits is that the inner mind's programs are way more powerful than the out of mind's desires. The second reason why "willpower" is "won't power" is that one of the major functions of the outer mind is to protect all inner mind programs. So the outer mind is in conflict with itself. On one hand, it wants to change a habit for all sorts of logical reasons and on the other hand, its marching orders are to run interference against any and all efforts to change that inner programming.

I'm not making this up. Ask anyone who has raised children. They can probably remember that up to about the age of 12, their kids would follow anything that they were told. Young kids would unquestioningly follow their parents over a cliff. At about the age of 12, they start responding to everything by putting their hands on their hips, looking up and asking, "Why?"

One of the marvels of human development is how the outer mind's primary role as the gatekeeper of the inner mind's programming changes as the child approaches very early teens. This role is mostly non-existent until that time so that all the inner minds can be taught the functioning it needs for life; toilet training, language, and morals. By early teens most of those tasks have been accomplished by their parents and society so, the outer mind will naturally evolve to its adult function as guardian of the inner mind's programming. This accounts for the "why" response. After that point, the inner mind only gets to experience new programming when the outer mind is circumvented by repetition, trauma, or hypnosis or self-hypnosis programming to the point where the inner mind now accepts the new action as the new normal and natural way.

Thus, there are two major ways of changing inner mind programming. The first utilizes self-hypnosis programming and the second, by doing a new habit consistently long enough for the inner mind to understand that this is the new way of doing things. Once the inner mind gets it, it will do the new thing habitually. For most minor habits, 30 days of consistently doing the new habit is usually enough for the inner mind to get the message and alter its programming. For major habits that have been practice for long periods of time, such as smoking or the one we are currently dealing with, loser thinking, it will probably take a longer period of practicing the new habit.

To effectively change habits this way takes an extraordinary amount of conscious awareness. There must be a constant vigilance of one's actions to make sure that the old habit does not slip or creep back in. Any temporary slips back into the old habit resets the timer of how long before the inner mind accepts new replacement habit (way of doing things) because the inner mind interprets the slip as, "Oh, I guess that new way was just temporary, so I have no reason to change."

Because people who have loser thinking will put themselves down and beat themselves up at the drop of a hat, I developed this new habit or practice that would counter that old one, one that could be done purposely and regularly.

> Most folks, who are in the habit of beating themselves up, love to do so in front of mirrors. If you catch yourself using the mirror to beat you up, you MUST reframe. You must say two positive nice things about you for every nasty one you utter or think and then you MUST smile. The best way to stop a habit is to replace it by doing another one more. Also, if one day you are not in the mood to smile or because you didn't usually smile you don't think you know how to, then fake it but you must smile every time you see you.
>
> What this exercise does is start a love affair between you and yourself, the foundation on which self-esteem is built. Once you have built up your esteem, you can truly become your own person and are on the way to personal happiness and success.

How do I know this is true? I originally developed this practice for me as I was the consummate loser thinker. I know it works and to this day, I still do it. And every client to whom I have taught it, reports the same results. A wonderful side benefit of this practice is that eventually your face becomes a trigger to an automatic smile, and you can't feel down or depressing yourself when you smile. So, if you are drinking as much water as you ought to, you'll have many opportunities to smile as you get rid of the excess water. If you happen to be in a funk as you're going to the bathroom, that automatic smile will break that state and you have a chance to have a wonderful rest of the day!

# Self-Confidence

For many years I confused self-esteem and self-confidence. I even at times in my writings and speech hyphenated them, "self-esteem/confidence". They are actually quite different. Whereas self-esteem is about one's insides, an evaluation of the qualities of self, self-confidence is one's evaluation about how well they can do things. How well they believe they can perform skills, tasks, actions, and exquisitely navigate the minefields of life. It's more of a general view of how likely you are to accomplish a goal, especially based on your experience.

As was covered in the section on the Self-Esteem/Love and the root cause of addictions, it is quite possible as well as quite disastrous, to have very high self-confidence and very low self-esteem/love.

The methods of acquiring both qualities are very different and although it is easier to build both qualities if the other one is fairly high, they operate in different parts of the inner mind and have different paths of development.

## My Prescriptions for Building Self-Confidence

### The Anchoring Technique

A great way to build self-confidence is through the use of anchoring, the mind's natural ability to tie an event or the feeling to one of the senses, visual, auditory, kinesthetic (touch, body sensory) and even taste and smell, primarily, though, visual, auditory and kinesthetic. If you think of your own experience, I am sure you can come up with examples where a song immediately transported you back to an event or a feeling tied to that event, where seeing a person immediately reminded you of someone you haven't thought about in years, or noticing when you tried on an old uniform, you stood taller and straighter just like you did when you wore that uniform for real. These examples and ones like them regularly happen in real life.

As with most NLP techniques, we're going to harness one of our natural abilities to accomplish the mission at hand. In this case we want to be able to capture the great feelings of a win after having accomplished something and store them away so that they will immediately become available for use in the future.

With this technique you're going to use both an auditory anchor and a kinesthetic one. The auditory anchor is saying the word, "YES!" used in an emphatic way and the kinesthetic anchor will be making a fist and pumping it in the air the same way an athlete would do upon having a win.

So, the full anchor is making a fist, pumping it up and down and at the same time saying, "YES!" If you're not comfortable with this particular set of anchors you are free to use ones of your own choosing, but this works well for most people because they naturally do this when they're exuberantly celebrating a win. The only caveat is that whatever you choose it can't be something that you would be doing regularly for other reasons.

There is a problem though; anchors will attach themselves to whatever is the strongest feeling, so before you use this anchor to overcome some negative self-confidence type feeling you have, you must make sure it is way stronger than the feelings you are attempting to overcome. Of course, we have a technique for strengthening these anchors. It's called *"stacking anchors."* If you were to use the exact same fist anchor technique to capture a 2$^{nd}$, 3$^{rd}$, 4$^{th}$, and 5$^{th}$ winning feeling, it would become stronger and stronger with each successive capture event.

Since most of us are in a hurry to have this anchor be strong enough to be useful so we can use it in our lives, we have a clever way of stacking anchors even without having to have experienced a real-life win. Fortunately, our inner minds do not have the ability to distinguish between real and imagined events. So if we imagine a situation where we won big and then on the next successive three exhaled breaths imagined that the feelings of that imagined win kept increasing and increasing until it was almost overpowering, If at that moment, you pumped your fist and said, emphatically "yes!" you would then have stacked another anchor on that fist.

Specifically, how do we pull off this clever little feat of fiction? Here are the directions:

1. Preferably, standing or at least sitting erect, Close your eyes.
2. Take a couple of slow, deep, breaths.
3. Picture in your mind's eye that you are now living the event where you are about to experience this outstanding achievement/win. This could be a performance, a speech, receiving a diploma, recognition of outstanding achievement from someone or organization, or doing whatever it is that we would like to use as a win.
    1. Just don't picture it, step into the picture and feel the great feelings and emotions, notice the surroundings (your office, the massive audience applauding you, the basketball you just threw making the winning points at the final buzzer, etc.) See yourself doing this activity and winning big time!
    2. While you are there, get all the senses working full-time by hearing the applause of the crowd, smelling the smells (if it's theatrical, greasepaint?), seeing our surroundings and what the people around us are doing (like applauding wildly). But most of all, tune in on how ecstatically you feel having just pulled off another amazing win!
    3. Now make sure that your physiology (the way you are standing or sitting, like back straight, head erect) is matching those great internal feelings.
    4. Now take a series of three slow, deep breaths and as you exhale each breath, notice that those great feelings double, then 10X, then 100X.
    5. When the feelings are about as good as they can get, make that fist anchor (or whatever one you chose) and say, emphatically, "Yes!"
    6. Congratulations, you now have another win in your self-confidence toolbox.

How would you use an anchor like this? Let's say you're about to perform, give a speech or make a presentation to your boss. In The Green Room or the bathroom or on the way into your boss's office you would just fire off this anchor by doing the same series of moves that you did to initially capture the feelings, in this case pumping a fist and saying yes. What will happen is all of those great wins that you put into that anchor will come flooding into your mind and totally overwhelm and vanquish any of the self-doubt that might have been lingering around, Then you can, with body erect and head held high, walk onto the stage, or podium or through the office door knowing fully that you are about to knock them dead!

Just remember that an anchor will attach itself to the strongest feeling or emotion so you need to build this one up hugely, by repeating the above exercise regularly and, even better, if you actually have a real win in your life, making sure that you capture those feeling by doing the anchor, before you use it to overcome negative ones.

**If You Can't, You Must! Technique**

Many years ago, when I was first starting my first rehab, I had to call on just about every official and community leader to the city to drum up support for my program. Most of these people I had never met, were very intimidating characters and in the beginning, with few introductions, I was forced to cold call them. Me, being just a grad student with a new, untested idea, the chances of getting a "no" from them was great.

I had a who's who list of people I needed to speak to. Sometimes I heard myself inventing reasons to call on them some other time. When that happened, I had a rule for myself that I had to immediately go call on them. If the result was a no, my other rule was that I had to call on two on the list for every no. The best way to change a habit (accepting defeat and giving up) is to do a new one more!

Although the anchoring technique is a quick way to build up self-confidence, at some point, this skill needs to be put into practice. For folks who have a history of little self-confidence, their fears of failure and other negative consequences have created avoidance habits including procrastination, making safe choices, creating depressive states and other avoidance behaviors. Without actually walking through the fears there will never be a win, so whenever you hear yourself making some flimsy excuse for inaction, like hearing yourself say, "I can't go or can't do that…" or notice procrastination, immediately think, "If I can't, I MUST!" and go and walk through the fears and get the win.

**Taking the Win Technique**

We discussed this technique as one that was useful for building self-esteem. It is also great for building self-confidence. For folks who are in the habit of picturing themselves as losing at life, there is a tendency to only notice things that support their limiting belief that they are no good. They will do everything possible to avoid recognizing evidence that would indicate that their view of their abilities was flawed, so when given recognition of a job well done or a compliment, they will dismiss it by explaining how "it was nothing special" or how the tie or piece of clothing was bought at a discount store, etc.

The only appropriate answer when being given a compliment is "Thank You" and then shut up! Anything else you say is going to diminish the compliment and robbing you of a win. You just got a free win without having to do any of that anchoring stuff, though, you can reinforce the win by, when you are next alone, doing that fist anchor to make it doubly yours.

If you regularly practice these exercises, there will be a time when you realize that you will be seeking out new and exciting opportunities to have new wins in your life. You will notice that you will automatically say yes to new things that in the past would have had you running to the exit. If you are a 12-Step person, you know that one of the principles is that you ought never refuse a 12-Step request. What I have just presented is the explanation for that practice.

**Self-Hypnosis Programming**

A great aid to increasing your self-confidence is to mentally practice doing things confidently. I developed a self-hypnosis program, originally to enhance my own confidence, that has been one of the all-time best sellers on my http://InnerGameTools. com website. You can purchase the download directly, though at https://gum.co/jjw204 Please read my directions on the order page before ordering it. Complete instructions are on the Inner Game Tools site.

# SECTION II

*Laying the Foundation for Well-Being*

# Understanding the Fundamentals of Alcoholism, Drug and Other Addictions and Prescriptions for Winning at Rehab and Other Remedial Endeavors

In the previous section, we explored the root cause of all addictions and most probably many of life's issues, self-esteem/love and to a lesser extent, self-confidence. In this section, I intend to focus on all the issues around addictions, including alcoholism and the non-chemical ones like co-dependency, gambling and overeating. As with most things in life, there are distinctions between occasional and habitual participation. I will explore that and then offer my take on how to overcome the habitual ones. Please enter into my presentation with an open mind. I will be discussing the use of the 12-Step programs, such as Alcoholics Anonymous and describe and explain the 12 Steps in detail. Please put aside all your preconceived notions about their usefulness until you have gotten my take on them. I assure you it is quite novel.

The battle plan here is to talk about how one can know to what degree they are dependent on addictive habits to get through life. Then my prescription to winning at rehab or for that matter, any serious remedial endeavor.

Finally, we will explore, in detail the 12 Steps, why they work from a therapeutic perspective and how to use them in your life.

## Alcohol, Drugs, And Other Addictions – How much is too much?

After forty years of experience in the substance abuse field, I have finally decided that there is a simple answer to the question of drugs and alcohol, 'how much is too much?' I will assume that a person asking this question of how much is too much is one that is looking to optimize his or her potential to grow emotionally and spiritually and to enjoy excellent mental health. My answer, therefore, is an optimum one.

The simple answer is that even one could be too much. Alcohol, drugs and other addictive habits are attractive because of their abilities to, in various ways, ease people through social and other situations, in lieu of having the experience of walking and working through the fears of those situations and growing from those experiences. The only thing learned, when using these substances, is that the cure for social ill-ease is using more of them.

I am sure that the majority of the people who use drugs and alcohol will never become addicted to a point where they will need professional assistance. I am just as sure that their emotional and social growth will be stunted in proportion to the degree of use. Much of what I do when I am working with former users, is to assist them to grow up emotionally. My rule of thumb is that when they started to depend on drugs and alcohol, their emotional growth stopped. If a person is now 38 years old and started to use at seventeen, the chances are that that person is dealing with the world from the emotional perspective of a seventeen-year-old. A disastrous situation, for instance, if that person happens to be a father of three or the CEO of a large corporation.

Everyone has the potential to be an addict or an alcoholic. Proclivity has a lot more to do with environmental factors than genetic ones. By environmental, I mean such things as how a person is taught as a child to cope with life; if friends and associates encourage and approve of use and abuse of mind altering substances; the frequency of opportunity for use; and, most important, how well they were taught and encouraged to like and feel good about themselves.

Very seldom, when listening to the life stories of recovering former addicts and alcoholics, do I hear that they were addicted after the first experience. They usually report that it was extremely pleasurable, and that the usage gradually increased until they crossed a line where stopping became a difficult or impossible task. Where that line is, is impossible to predict and is different for each person. What is insidious is that the process happens so gradually that only in retrospect, after stopping, is it even apparent that such a line even existed. This is why I believe that using drugs and alcohol at any level, even "recreationally" can be the equivalent of recreationally juggling dynamite.

My mind has been conducting a debate with itself as I have been writing this section. The debate is between the part that cries out for a moderate liberal stance and the absolutist part, which has been doing the writing up to now. The liberal part argues that there is nothing wrong with having an occasional glass of wine with dinner, or an occasional marijuana joint after dinner or at a party, and that a person who might have a drink or a joint once a week is running a very small risk of becoming an alcoholic or a drug addict.

The absolutist part concedes that the chances are really slim. It then suggests that if that occasional drink just happens to occur on "special occasions" like dinner with an important client or that joint just happens to be smoked when first getting to know a new love interest and that the drink or joint sort of takes the edge of the tension of the moment, like it's supposed to, then, at the least, it is impeding the person's learning how to relax and walk through such situations. At the worst, it is letting the person's sub-conscious, or as I now like to call it, "the inner mind," know of a really neat way of not having to deal with similar tensions.

The inner mind does not know pasts and futures and just accumulates experience in the present tense. For this reason, each of these "occasional experiences" become an increasingly more powerful alternative solution that the inner mind knows it can call on. For the person who ends up as an alcoholic or an addict, the inner mind does call on that alternative with increasing frequency, while justifying it, consciously, as "just an occasional drink". That is what the process of denial is all about.

So, the absolutist part still insists that none is best and those who dabble infrequently should still be aware of the risks.... I, the judge in this debate, matched up the arguments with my experience and agree with the absolutist part. I think it would be irresponsible to give anyone the assurance that alcohol or drugs in any quantity is effect or risk free.

I also feel the need to point out that the infrequent users of marijuana are probably at the greatest risk since it is unlikely that they will just take one toke of the substance. They will, usually, smoke until the euphoria is felt (usually referred to as "being stoned"). The equivalent of this in drinking terms would be if the occasional drinkers drank until they were drunk.

The euphoria of being stoned is a powerful experience for the inner mind. What makes marijuana even more potentially addictive is that, since there is little chance of there being any negative physical side effects, gradually increased usage can be easily rationalized under the guise of fun or, at least, the absence of any obvious negatives.

Marijuana is the only substance where people who are addicted to it have no realization of just how much it controls their lives until they stop using for a while and look backward. Marijuana addicts seem to themselves to be operating super-functionally, when in fact the opposite is true.

As I stated in the beginning, I am writing from the point of view of how to get the most out of one's life experience.

> The Self-Test Challenge: For a period of a month, abstain from all mind-altering substances; drugs, alcohol, poppers, all of them, while you carry on your life as usual. Go to your business lunches, your first dates, your cocktail parties, do all the sex-type things you normally do, and make that after dinner speech. The only thing that will be different is that you will be doing everything without alcohol and/or drugs.
>
> My bottom-line advice for the person who insists on using alcohol and/or drugs recreationally is to be ruthlessly honest with themselves by doing the above self-test challenge at least once, preferably twice, a year.

If your use of drugs and/or alcohol is strictly a recreational want and not a need or dependence, then you find no difference in your stress or tension level when you do all those activities drug and alcohol free. If you experience increased stress and tension, it is a sign that, for the activities where the increases are noticed, you have been relying on those substances to get you through. The more stress and tension noticed, the more you are relying on them and the greater the risk of becoming dependent on them. This gives you a way to decide for yourself what level of usage is right for you. I am not saying "don't use", just keep your eyes open to what is going on and then make your decisions.

If you cannot stay alcohol and drug free for the entire length of the test period, you either are, or are about to be in serious trouble. Incidentally, if you are actually someone who is using mind-altering substances addictively and has been denying to yourself that fact, your mind will come up with all sorts of good reasons why it is O.K. to stop this test prematurely or, maybe even why there is no need to even take it in the first place. So, for the purposes of this test, there are zero reasons to start using your mind-altering goodies again before the entire period you committed to before the test started is over. If you refuse to even consider taking the abstinence test, you might already be in deep water.

It is my experience that people who are addicted to mind-altering substances build huge walls of denial to rationalize their continued use. Occasionally, addicts and alcoholics will have a moment of clarity, when it will become obvious how addicted they really are. These moments sometimes occur immediately following a particularly bad experience, such as an overdose. At other times, it can be just a spontaneous insight after reading an article such as this one. These moments of clarity are truly "moments" and if assistance is not sought out quickly, the window of opportunity will slam shut as the rationales and denials come flooding back in.

If you can relate to this last section, please seek assistance quickly for it might be a painfully long time before your next opportunity. You can call your local Alcoholics Anonymous, Narcotics Anonymous, Cocaine Anonymous, Crystal Meth Anonymous, Marijuana Anonymous offices. Call information and ask for their central offices. It is also probably a good idea to seek out the assistance of a certified addiction counselor, like me, to walk you through this process.

## How to Win the Rehab Game Without Gaming the System

Having read the last section and having decided that you really could use some assistance to learn how to live life on life's terms without the assistance of any addictive goodies or habits, here are my suggestions on how to most efficiently approach the rehab process. Actually, these suggestions apply to any learning endeavor.

For those of you who are reading this because you think that I am going to give you a method to make rehab easy so that you can slide right through, hassle-free, you are right but not the way you think you are right. What I am about to present is a way to get through rehab in the shortest amount of time and emerge on the other side with the tools and the skills to begin the journey to a wonderful life.

If you thought that by titling this "How to Win the Game" I meant "How to Game the System" you couldn't be more wrong.

If you are an alcoholic or drug addict, you are already an expert at gaming the system. If you are now entering a rehab after a successful career of gaming the system, you know how well, being successful at gaming the system really works for the quality and welfare of your life. There is an old rehab saying, "The cheater cheats him/herself!" That is why when you are successful at gaming the system, you lose at the game of life. When you are an expert at gaming the system, you also become an expert at gaming yourself. You lie to yourself so often that you believe your own lies. You take the easier, less painful way instead of choosing a path based on what will be a winning method because you tell yourself that it will work even in the face of overwhelming evidence that it has never worked before. You choose it because you choose anything that is less painful. That is why doing more of whatever it was that got you to the door of rehab became the immediate answer to most painful problems.

When you scam the system you usually scam yourself in the process. So when I say I am going to teach you how to win the rehab game, I really mean how to WIN! If you follow these simple suggestions, you will have a tough but easy time in rehab and you will get through it and on to the rest of your life in record time.

How do I know this is true? Because I have been in this rehab game for a long, long time. I have worked in just about every part of the rehab game from being a counselor to starting and running residential rehabs and have managed to have lived a life without needing or wanting to use any of my old goodies for over forty years. I know what I am about to teach you works because

I have personally witnessed hundreds of folks just like you work their way through the rehab game. I am a keen observer. I noticed what those folks did while they were in rehab, who got through rehab in record time and learned all they needed to have the tools to build a great life,

I also watched all the others who tried to do rehab the same way they did their life when they were using. They lied, to themselves and to the staff, and lots of the time actually got away with it. The problem is that when they lied and took the shortcuts they never grew inside and never learned the tools that are so necessary for life outside of rehab. They didn't understand that rehab is just a rehearsal for life after rehab. It is time out from the real world where there are usually heavy consequences for goofing up and making lousy choices. They didn't understand that in rehab, they could have the freedom to make wrong choices and just get the feedback they need to learn what choices really work, without having to risk anything. Many of these folks actually were good enough at lying and cheating and scamming that they gave the appearance of having gotten all they needed to get out of rehab and graduated. The problem is that they were all appearance and no substance. The cheater cheats himself!

Then once again used all their cunning skills of their using life to give the illusion of having learned the lessons by feeding back to the staff all the right answers and doing all the right actions that the staff expected without doing any of the tough work on the inside. So when they graduated and went out in the real world with real consequences, they did not have the tools they needed to both survive and thrive. They probably also were running the same game on their sponsors, if they even bothered to get one, and quickly turned to some form of addiction once again.

**Two suggestions to really win at the rehab game:**

**Radical honesty**

Become ultra-honest with yourself and admit that you don't have the foggiest clue as to what to do next. This is the process that all winners do and all people who don't win never do. It is the most important thing that one must do to win at any game that involves learning new skills to win. It is very simple while being painfully difficult at the same time. Only when you know that you don't know, are you ready to hear and do whatever it is you are being taught. If you have accepted that you do not know the answer because you have tried doing it the ways you have always done it and ended up without success, then you will be finally open to suggestion and direction. You will finally become teachable!

**Know That You Don't Know**

Without getting to the point that you know that you do not know, what happens is that you are given a suggestion and you reject it without ever doing it. You will have a thousand reasons why it won't work, and all of those reasons based on what? Oh yes, with your old thinking which worked so well that you are now in rehab. Get it? Your old thinking patterns got you to rehab. The reason for being in rehab is to learn new patterns of thinking that will really serve you. If you have gut-level, gotten that your best thinking when you were using got you to nowhere except to rehab (possibly via jails and loony bins) then you will put your ideas of what sounds good aside and be open to not only hear new suggestions, you will actually follow through and actually do the suggestions and notice the results of doing the suggested work .

I can always tell who has accepted, gut-level, that they know that they do not know. They jump on every suggested course of action and put it into action without question and then check

JASON WITTMAN, MPS, LAADC, CATC-IV

out the results. Those who have not yet accepted that they do not have the answers and are still under the self-illusion that they are smarter than their teachers, don't do the work and instead spend their precious time in rehab, punching holes in everything except their own baloney. They will have a thousand reasons why a suggestion will not work, without ever doing the work.

When I kept getting reasons why what I was suggesting wasn't going to work, I have actually said to counselees of mine, "If you know so much about what works and does not work, how come it is that you are sitting in that chair (the resident in a rehab chair) and I am sitting in this one?" When you hear yourself questioning a suggestion from someone who obviously knows more than you do on a subject before you actually do the suggestion and check out the results that doing the suggestion brings you, you need to remember that if you knew the solution you would not have asked the question. So, shut up and go do the work!

So far, the focus has been on developing the self, both the inner self-esteem self and the outer self-confident self. These are the fundamental skills that must be mastered to be able to operate successfully in a world that includes other people, places, and things.

If you have embraced what I have written so far and are actually doing the work without reservation and excuses, then you have finished the preliminary work on the 1st of the 12 steps, for I believe that the essence of that step and the intended outcome of working that step is coming to the understanding that your best thinking hasn't worked and that you know that you do not know. If you understand that, you are now teachable and are well on the way to winning at the rehab game!

## Why the 12 Steps Work... and why they are valuable adjunct to therapeutically working with recovering people - A Therapeutic Explanation

I am often asked why I believe the 12 Steps work. There are two ways to arrive at a belief. The first is through dogma, "I've been instructed; therefore, I believe." The second is through doubt, "I question it and still, after doing them, I get good results." For me, it was the latter. I got clean and sober because I started a residential therapeutic community (TC) for drug addicts, Alpha House, while I still was in grad school at Cornell University in Ithaca, NY. It was an abstinent program, so I became abstinent. My original motivation for starting it was as a do-gooder being of service. As time went on, I realized I probably ought to have been in it rather than running it, so I paid good attention. Therapeutic communities did not teach the 12 Steps, so I was unaware of them. Also, at the time, Alcoholics Anonymous was unwelcoming to those with drug problems, so I never explored it.

Many years later, in Los Angeles and working with street kids, I had one with whom I couldn't get to stop drinking and my best counseling stuff wasn't working. Because he was a pure alcoholic who had never used drugs, in desperation, I offered to take him to AA. He said OK.

Because I had never been to an AA meeting, I decided to familiarize myself so I could be a good guide for him. I went to a meeting to scope it out. To my relief, most people were calling themselves addicts and alcoholics, so I decided AA had come of age and I paid attention. When I looked up on the wall, there were the 12 Steps. I realized that I had been doing them already but I didn't know they had an order. It seems that the model for the program I started in Ithaca was originally developed by guys who left AA when they felt not welcomed as addicts and started Synonon in Venice, California. Obviously, they took the 12 Steps with them and incorporated them into the program they developed.

The kid, for whom I scoped out AA, took another 6 months to get there, but I stayed because I thought it was a good support group for me. To make sure I got it down well, even with 8 years sober, I went to 365 meetings in as many days, got a sponsor, and worked through the Steps. 44+ years later, I guess that was a good investment.

As a therapist, albeit an unconventional one, I can explain why the Steps are useful for good mental health:

**Step 1:** "We admitted we were powerless over alcohol – that our lives had become unmanageable."

Without coming to the realization that "my best thinking does little more than produce lousy results" one isn't ready to even attempt new ideas. Only after accepting the reality of an inability to conjure up a workable solution to a problem, will one become teachable.

When I am working with clients and they are telling me why my suggestions will not work for them before they attempt to do them, 1st Step bells go off in my head reminding me the futility of making any further suggestions before we revisit just why I am being asked for counseling.

**Step 2:** "Came to believe that a Power greater than ourselves could restore us to sanity."

It is a useful visualization to have a 3rd party, a force, that somehow is karmically providing strength and cover when needed. This is a Step that usually starts out with doubtful acceptance and, with experience, becomes an accepted belief. For those who don't buy the God stuff, a recognition that the universe seems to be pretty well organized and that life just might be easier to cope with if one can embrace the assumption that that Universe could be tapped into for moral assistance at difficult times. Broadly speaking, many folks have found that the 12 Step fellowship can become a viable temporary substitute for God until one of their understanding can be developed and embraced. Although nice if one can adopt some concept here, it is not an essential part of the effectiveness of the rest of the Steps. It is quite OK to doubt this one and move on.

Many people have been able to find "a God of their understanding" by taking the saying literally and designing then conceptualizing what such a God would do, look like, act and feel. Then, they use this well-formed image as a temporary God substitute, understanding that the definition and concept will change and evolve through experience.

**Step 3:** "Made a decision to turn our will and our lives over to the care of God *as we understood Him*."

I view this step as a two-part one, I do the footwork in front of me, and I turn overall responsibility for the results of my footwork to the Universe (God, or whatever, as long as it isn't me). This is basically a recognition of reality. Once I have done all the footwork I can do, it is a waste of energy to continue kvetching, worrying, and speculating about the results. When I get the results (aka, feedback) I then and only then, know what my next footwork ought to be. Until then, it is none of my business, so I go on to other footwork I need to do. Since I have accepted this concept, I have lived a 98% anxiety-free life. Since anxiety is just fear of future results and since I trust that that is 100% God's responsibility, then the anxiety disappears.

**Step 4** "Made a searching and fearless moral inventory of ourselves." & **Step 5:** "Admitted to God, to ourselves and to another human being the exact nature of our wrongs."

The inner mind (sometimes called the unconscious mind) does not know pasts and futures. It only knows and operates in the present. It does know complete from incomplete. These steps allow the inner mind to view the past as completed action, so emotions from the past stop clouding the creative process. When this happens, new and useful thought and action have a chance of taking root. Only then can the mind produce constructive and life-fulfilling action. (I, personally, write a 4th Step once a year to clear out any accumulated emotional garbage that wasn't taken care of by my nightly 10th Step writing.)

This two-step process does a more effective job of clearing out years of accumulated emotional garbage than most of the formal therapeutic processes. Once these steps are completed, the risk of relapse is drastically reduced. Until these steps are completed, a newly recovering person's good feelings are mainly a combination of the honeymoon effect and hitchhiking on the good feelings of those with long-term recovery. Most people who slip in their first year of being substance-free do so because they have not completed their 5th step and internally they still have that historical emotional pain and start to think that since there is no improvement they ought to go and do what they know will bring instant relief.

There are many ways of writing a 4th Step and I emphasize that this is a writing exercise. While the 5th Step absolutely needs a Sponsor or another trusted person to hear you read the 4th Step writing, if you do not yet have a Sponsor, you can still do the writing. Many people will do this writing as it is laid out in the Big Book of AA. Other will use various guides. I developed a most thorough and complete one of my own. It is based on an old guide I found somewhere and that over the years have elaborated and improved on with new insights and understandings I have acquired along the way. You can find a downloadable copy of it on my website at: http://stage2recovery.com/my-forth-step-guide/ or https://bit.ly/st4guide

**Step 6:** "Were entirely ready to have God remove all these defects of character." **& Step 7:** "Humbly asked Him to remove all these defects of character."

These Steps address changing old non-functional and irresponsible habits and limiting beliefs. The 6th Step is the preparatory one that involves making a list of all the things one would want to change and become willing to forgo the secondary benefits and payoffs associated with them. **The 7th Step** is actually making the changes.

**Step 8:** "Made a list of all persons we had harmed and became willing to make amends to them all." **& Step 9:** "Made direct amends to such people wherever possible, except when to do so would injure them or others."

Again the 8th Step is the preparatory one where the person makes a list of all those people that have been wronged including oneself and, again, becoming willing to follow through with making amends. The 9th Step is actually making amends in a responsible and thoughtful way. This set of Steps addresses head-on, the resolution of guilt and shame. After doing these Steps and the 4th and 5th ones, most accumulated bad feelings are resolved and for the first time for many, there is a feeling of comfort and joy. There will usually be a noticeable change in emotion and guilt-driven behavior and thinking with a corresponding shift in outlook and perspectives.

**Step 10:** "Continued to take personal inventory and when we were wrong promptly admitted it."

This is a daily tool to make sure that steps 3 through 9 are continually practiced which will keep the emotional gut from accumulating new crap. Later on, I will be describing a great method of doing automatic writing. It works very will for 10th step writing. I have a 5" x 8" spiral notebook with a pen stored in the spiral that sits on my bed where I do my 10th step writing every night as I have every night for the past 26+ years.

**Step 11:** "Sought through prayer and meditation to improve our conscious contact with God as we understood Him, praying only for knowledge of His will for us and the power to carry that out."

JASON WITTMAN, MPS, LAADC, CATC-IV

Meditation, in whatever its form, has been scientifically shown to be highly beneficial when practiced daily. I did Tai Chi for many years. William Glasser, MD in his book, "Positive Addiction" surveyed many successful people and found that the one thing they all had in common was they all did some daily mindless activity (jogging without music or conversation, chanting, Tai Chi, yoga, swimming, etc.) for at least a half an hour. He speculated that this was useful in that it gave the inner mind a time when it didn't need to watch out for and control the body and could just free-associate and be creative.

**Step 12:** "Having had a spiritual awakening as the result of these steps, we tried to carry this message to alcoholics, and to practice these principles in all our affairs."

One of the most effective ways to keep a practice is to pass it on to and teach it to others. After I had been doing the art for over 10 years, my Tai Chi Master suggested that I start teaching. I didn't and eventually, I stopped remembering the forms and stopped doing it. When I am teaching the Steps to newcomers, there is a little voice that sits on my right shoulder by my right ear that occasionally whispers to me, "That was nice what you just suggested for him to do, are you doing that in *your* life?"

So, I hope the reader can understand from this brief tour, these Steps are a fairly good prescription for clearing out the emotional baggage of the past and a guide to address new feelings and behavior as they occur to maintain an emotionally positive life.

## Here are Some of the Added Benefits of 12 Step Programs

Twelve Step programs offer a lot more than just the above Steps, which of themselves are supremely beneficial. These programs offer two additional features that make them of even greater value to recovering folks. They offer a fellowship of ultra-supportive people all of whom are walking the same path and are motivated to be supportive by the Twelfth Step. A very important sub-part of this fellowship is the concept of sponsorship. A sponsor is someone with years of experience with doing the 12 Steps who serves as a teacher, mentor, and coach for the newly recovering person. Once the Steps have been taught and done, the sponsor becomes a trusted advisor who can be called on to assist in applying the Steps to daily life and life's foibles. This is a perfect,

positive example of how "The Environment Always Wins!"

## Portability

One of the problems I experienced working therapeutically with recovering people prior to my introduction to 12 Step programs was that if the client left the area or even in between therapeutic sessions there was little or no outside, ongoing support. Also, without a positive support group, even those who remained in the area after their therapy was complete would be going back to and associating with the same people and in the same environment that they formally use in. The Environment Always Wins, so those who go back to a using environment and using buddies will, most likely, eventually succumb. The 12 Step programs are the only programs that I know of, which offer a supportive, positive, cost-free environment virtually 24/7 and worldwide. For this feature alone, getting your clients (or if you are reading this for your own benefit, getting you) involved will greatly assure that your good therapeutic work with them will survive and continue to grow long after your work is done.

## Building Social Graces

The other important feature of these programs is an emphasis on Service. There are many opportunities in every meeting for members of be of service, from being a greeter at the door to being the meeting secretary who is responsible for the meetings' smooth operation. Plus, there are speakers at most meetings who are members with more experience. All these opportunities assist the members to build both self-esteem and self-confidence.

Building a strong sense of self-esteem/love is one of the best relapse prevention practices.

Although the following paragraph is written with addiction counselors in mind, if you are a person beginning your recovery process, this is a pretty good summary of the benefits of becoming a member of a 12 Step program.

If you are a therapist or a counseling professional, I hope this brief survey of the feature of 12 Step programs from a therapeutic point of view will assist your understanding of how getting your clients/patients involved in these programs would be a valuable adjunct to your therapeutic efforts. With programs I design, therapy plays a critically important role along with teaching and coaching the skills of living life successfully after drugs and alcohol. Encouraging client involvement in 12 Step programs both allows the therapist to address issues that are uncovered through the working of the Steps and the resocialization issues as they integrate into those groups and most importantly, provides a continually supportive environment that allows the therapy and life-skills training to flourish.

## Why the "Relapse" Concept is a Setup for Disaster

*Labeling a decision to return to old behaviors as "Relapse" is counterproductive to the behavior change process.*

The standard definition of "relapse" is a return to an active disease state after a period of remission, sometimes referred to as recovery. The problem with all these terms when they are used in the context of addictions is that they are being used to describe a condition that is primarily a very ingrained habit as if it was an incurable disease.

*For the sake of this discussion, I am defining an addiction (including an alcohol one) as a mal-adaptive behavior chosen by individuals to cope with emotional pain that, through both repeated usage and the initially pleasurable aspects of the behavior, becomes an ingrained habit. If those behaviors involve physically addictive and painful-to-stop substances, the avoidance of the pain of stopping (withdrawals) will, in itself, reinforce the habit.*

The process of becoming addicted starts with personal choice. There was some sort of unfulfilled need within individuals that seemed to be satisfied by their initial experimentation with the behavior. At that point there was a choice to continue that behavior because it was producing the desired relief from their internal pains. With any behavior, repeated use will eventually signal to the Inner Mind (subconscious) that the behavior is normal and natural so the Inner Mind will adopt it as the standard operating procedure and will produce that behavior on cue. At that point, the behavior is now a habit. The longer that habit is practiced, the more ingrained it will become. What started out as a choice has now become an automatic process and will stay that way until another choice to the contrary is made.

Because some of these habitual behaviors involve substances that are physically addictive with real withdrawal symptoms associated with stopping their usage, this whole process of behavior change has been labeled by the medical world as a disease and all the disease metaphors have been applied to it.

There are actually two things going on here, a physical addiction and an ingrained habit that have been conflated into one disease concept. Because of that, the focus becomes treating a disease rather than that of changing a habit. Also, by using disease metaphors, especially the "incurable" ones, it is a set up for returning to the old behavior. The meta message for the term "relapse" is that going back to old behaviors is a normal and natural part of the cycles of recovery. That might be true for cancer, but with the changing of ingrained habits, it is just a convenient excuse for choosing to return to a former behavior. The problem is, it becomes a pattern and a set up for future repeats of those lousy decisions.

There is no such thing as failure. It's just feedback! Something new needs to be learned. Labeling a decision to pick up an old habit again as relapsing just reinforces self-blame and shame instead of just acknowledging it as a lousy decision, figuring out what lessons were missed, making the necessary corrections, and moving on. There is no shame is owning having made a poor choice, learning how to do better and choosing to do those better things, no matter what.

## Looking at Recovery Process from a Habit Change Perspective

1.   Through progressive, negative experiences that can be associated with what was here-to-fore pleasurable activities, a realization emerges that continued practice of the behavior is producing an unmanageable life and that something needs to change, though how to do that might be a mystery.
2.   They made a choice to stop the behavior and seek a better solution and as long as there is a hope that that will happen, they will stay stopped. This is actually a very powerful choice because normally the Outer Mind just carries out the automatic programming of the Inner Mind. When that programming is producing nothing but continued grief, the Outer Mind overrides that programming and stops the behavior.
3.   As they learn new and more effective ways of dealing with those inner hurts and as the time since the last practice of the old behavior increases, the Inner Mind starts to get the message that these new behaviors are the normal and natural thing to do and that becomes the new ingrained habit.
4.   So, what explains the process of returning to the old behavior?

a.  They get a stray thought of "wouldn't it be nice to do........."

b.  They choose to ignore all their past history and their Inner Voice that knows and tells them that this is a foolish move. Part of this choice might be that they have not gotten enough good feelings out of this new behavior change process fast enough to satisfy their need for relief, so they give up prematurely.

c.  They choose to continue through all the precursor steps that eventually result in doing the old behavior again.

d.  They choose to use. To excuse this choice by labeling it as a relapse, as if some evil disease grabbed them and caused them to do things they didn't want to do, is a less than useful description of this process. And what is worse, it feeds into that choice to use by providing the excuse that this is just what addicts and alcoholics do in early recovery. It fails to recognize the ability to choose one's behaviors. It totally ignores that God gave us the powerful ability to learn from past experiences and to choose to do things differently. That is the process of becoming a responsible adult.

e.  The final prevention step would be to explore what added change in thinking or behaviors might be needed to ensure that any possible cause for reverting to old behaviors would be eliminated. With the root cause of all addictions being low or no self-esteem/love, the chances are that redoubling the efforts to build a great self-evaluation of one's being, i.e., self-esteem/love, would be the best solution.

JASON WITTMAN, MPS, LAADC, CATC-IV

# People Will Gravitate Towards Happiness and Away from Pain

The "attraction" reference in the AA Traditions is all about selling new people on eventual happiness. The laughter and success stories in the meeting are the best demonstration of that happiness. The problem is that if newer people do not quickly experience those feelings in themselves, the pull to chase the temporary happiness of their former behavior can drive them to once again choose to relive their past. For all people new to this process, it is a race against time to ensure that they get to the point where their new great feelings will override any stray "wouldn't it be nice…" thoughts.

A very important takeaway is that people will gravitate towards happiness and away from pain.

When people make the choice to stop their destructive habits they are doing so in a quest for a new happiness. Most behavioral choice is driven by that principle.

In early AA, there was a push to do all 12 Steps in the first couple of months. I think they had it right. Added to that, of course, the enhancing of their self-esteem/love makes this a totally winning process.

## Why We Do Things That We Know Are Not in Our Best Interests

In almost every culture, there is a teaching tale that gives guidance about how to deal with the inclination to do things that are not in our best interest and that deep inside we know is bad juju.

In a Native American teaching tale, there is the old man who tells his grandson about the two wolves that live inside everyone. The good wolf who wants one to succeed and be happy and the evil one that keeps getting in the way and tearing down one's self-esteem. The child asks the old man, "Which one wins?" The grandfather's reply is, "The one you feed."

In the 12 Step traditions, the principle is about the fight between the self-will and the God-driven guidance. They talk about "Self Will Run Riot!"

In Jewish mysticism, the Kabbalah, the evil wolf is called the "yetzer hara" which translates as "the evil inclination." It tries to overpower the "yetzer hatov," the inclination to do good. Actually, in the Jewish tradition, the difference is not just good vs. evil but more that the yetzer hatov is like a well-formed conscience. It isn't that it vanquishes the evil inclination but rather it keeps it in check by continually reminding the person of what is their higher purpose. They then can make responsible, adult choices rather than giving in to the impulse towards property, pleasure, prestige, and security. All those things are not bad on their own. The problem is that if done to the extreme, will lead to either personal and/or societal evil and/or self-destruction.

In my research on this concept, I believe I discovered why in the Jewish religion, a young person at the age of 13 is considered an adult in the Jewish community. Within the Bar Mitzvah (Bat Mitzvah, for girls) there is a meta-message, "OK, kid, it is time for you to start acting with adult values. We will still be here to guide you but now you have the responsibility of learning these adult things." I had always thought that it was a recognition of the ability to function as an adult and make decisions as an adult. The religious teachings recognize that. They argue, though, that the ability to now function as an adult is attributed to a 13-year-old's newly developed ability to intuitively know right from wrong, right thinking and action of what might be good in the long run from always choosing instant gratification or pleasure. They talk about the first 13 years of a child's life being ruled by yetzer hara with the moderating force coming from the outside in the form of parental or societal controls. In early adolescence, the yetzer hatov becomes increasingly more developed until, at around 13 years old, it can begin to assume the responsibility of self-moderating the influence of their yetzer hara.

I really like this concept because it explains how adults continually make choices that are not in their best self-interest. When they do not have a strongly developed yetzer hatov, the inclination to do good, they consistently give in to their yetzer hara. This applies to all those dilemmas where their actions override their common (or not so common) sense, from procrastination to ultimately resuming their addictions.

For people who have made a career out of doing things, not in their or society's best interest, they have gotten in the habit of feeding the evil wolf, within. They have taken the easier, softer way of letting their yetzer hara, control their decisions and their lives and all the addictions, isms and negativity rule.

The bottom line, here, is the choice to follow either one's yetzer hara (evil inclination) or yetzer hatov (the inclination to do good) is a matter of which one is the stronger habit and that is controlled by which one is practiced more. If one has the practice of following their yetzer hatov or inclination to choose the responsible and life-fulfilling thought and action, they will automatically modify, moderate and/or overpower their yetzer hara.

The only way to have such a practice is to practice! There is an old theatrical story of a student asking how to get to Carnegie Hall, the premier performance space of its day. The answer was, "practice, practice, practice!" The only way to change a habit is to do the one you want more than the old one. That means, in the beginning, one needs consciously, deliberately and with every ounce of energy they can muster up, to override the old habit of giving into their yetzer hara. Once their inner mind gets that the new way of doing things (aka the new habit) is to follow the yetzer hatov, the inclination toward good, then, for the most part, choices become effortless and automatic and the possibility of winning at life is extremely good.

## Planning on Stopping Smoking or Other Not So Good Habits?

For some strange reason, at the beginning of a new year, or milestone events like birthdays, human beings go through a curious ritual of making resolutions to change those things that didn't work out during the just concluded year. The problem is that they might have all sorts of good intentions when they make those resolutions, but they lack most of the internal tools to keep the resolve up long enough to have any success. It's one thing to acknowledge that a behavior has not been working for our best behalf and it's another thing to let go of that behavior and all the short-term goodies, sometimes referred to as secondary gains, that were derived from that behavior. It's the biggest thing of all to actually make the changes.

For most folks, this won't be the first time that they made these same resolutions. After many attempts that ended in failure, there is a part of their inner mind that is as negatively powerful as the undesirable behavior. That part has a voice that says, "So what is going to be different this time? It doesn't matter what you do, it's just going to end in disaster as usual." Variations of this mantra will show up in one's internal conversations. Sometimes it will manifest itself nonverbally as defeatist behaviors such as procrastination or flat-out giving up. One way or another, unless that part becomes convinced that the desired change is winnable, it will sabotage all efforts.

Although the following is directed towards successfully eliminating tobacco use, the methods and principles described apply to and can be used to tackle changing other habits.

**The Resolution to Quit Tobacco**

One of the most resolutioned behaviors is the use of tobacco products. These days with fewer people smoking, a more health-conscious population whose tolerance for second-hand smoke is at an all-time low, and smoking banned from all public places and public transportation, the external pressure is on to stop. External pressures, on their own, are not usually enough to get one to resolve to stop. But all that pressure on top of becoming aware of the deteriorating condition of their lungs, as evidenced by smoker's coughs and frequent colds, makes it hard to ignore that nagging feeling that maybe the jig is up and that they had better quit now before it is too late.

What follows are some concrete suggestions for how to use your mind to successfully assist you to once and for all win the resolution game.

*Note:* Although I am using stopping the use of tobacco products as the example, the suggestions are equally applicable to any habit you might want to change.

Tobacco is the perfect drug. Its ingredients are both a stimulant, nicotine, and a calmative agent, acetaldehyde (the first metabolite of alcohol and the probable cause of hangovers). It is a literal smoke screen and it gives one something to do with hands. What more could you want? Well, maybe, the ability to breathe fully and live long. The problem is that those are long term goals and they are usually trumped by short term gains because the emotional costs of giving up those short-term gains are too painful to withstand. Until the cost of the short-term gains become too high or are satisfied by other means, smoking will remain as an entrenched habit.

If you are one of those who is resolved to be successful this time, here are a couple of my most useful tips:

## Nicotine Patches

A lot of folks use nicotine replacement aids, like the patch, to make the process easier. If you are going to be using patches or some other type of nicotine replacement source like nicotine gum, you should know the physical addiction to nicotine would be over in a matter of weeks if one was to just quit cold turkey. They work. The main reason they work has less to do with withdrawing from the nicotine -- the body will be detoxed after a couple of weeks of abstinence -- than giving the inner mind three months to get used to functioning without the physical act of smoking.

The main reason why the course of treatment with patches lasts for three months is three-fold. The first is that reducing the amount of nicotine in the system in increments gradually makes it less of a jolt to the system than cold turkey. A sudden jolt could produce sufficient anxiety to trigger the urge to resume smoking.

Furthermore, an even more important second reason why the patches are used for three months has to do with the other part of smoking, the secondary gains or payoffs. There will be a three-month break from the physical habit of smoking during which time the person will have the opportunity to develop new behaviors that will more responsibly satisfy those needs.

A third and most important reason has to do with how the inner, or subconscious, mind works.

The inner mind will automatically carry out whatever programs it thinks are normal and natural. After smoking for an extended length of time, the inner mind thinks that smoking is the normal program and will do everything it can to carry that program out. The longer one stays away from the physical act of smoking the better the chance of the inner mind understanding that just breathing air is the new normal program. Once it gets that this is the new program, the urge to smoke will be gone.

It is very important to understand the concept that the longer the time away from the physical act of smoking, the more solid will be the inner mind's adoption of the new behavior. Many people will have a cigarette every once in a while, during the three months of the nicotine patch program. Every time they do that, they are effectively starting from scratch in the campaign to get the inner mind to adopt the new behavior. When I'm coaching folks who are using nicotine substitutes to stop smoking, I have found that the success rate is way lower for those who occasionally smoked during the three months than for those who stayed cigarette free.

Regardless of what method one uses to stop smoking, those who daily visualize about their new tobacco-free lives have the most success.

The easiest way to do this type of visualization is to make yourself comfortable in an environment where you will not be disturbed. Take some nice, deep breaths letting them out slowly. As you take the breaths in, notice the parts of your body that are a bit tense and tighten the muscles in those areas even more. Then, as you let the breaths out, let those muscles relax. Doing that regularly will teach the inner mind to associate slow, deep breaths with body relaxation.

If you have problems with this exercise, please use my free MP3 download that you will be able to download at https://gumroad.com/l/jjw201/comp1

## How to Structure Visualizations and Affirmations

The other oddity of how the inner mind operates is that it drops out of the sentence any negative modifiers, such as "not." If you were to visualize "I am in this social situation where in the past

I would have always smoked and now I am not smoking..." the inner mind will drop the word "not" out of that sentence and will hear it as "and now I am smoking." Since English is usually spoken in negatives and double negatives, i.e.: "He is not unkind," it really takes practice to be able to do a visualization totally using positive descriptors.

What you imagine gets realized! There is a famous study of basketball players practicing free throws where one group physically practiced doing free throws for a period of time while another group did not do anything physical -- instead, only repeatedly visualized making perfect free throws. The group that did the visualization had the most improvement! This works, and if you regularly visualize a life beyond tobacco, you will greatly up the chances of success.

Until the inner mind understands that smoking and the use of tobacco products is a thing of the past, thoughts will regularly occur that call for and urge you to indulge. Since it is impossible to block anything from one's mind, the easiest way to deal with these thoughts is to acknowledge that they are there and thank that part of you that keeps bringing it up for sharing. Then remember what you were doing before the thought and go back to doing it. For persistent urges, when that voice won't shut up, I suggest using the following NLP technique:

Since most people compartmentalize their mind when they describe what's going on inside by giving each part a voice as in, "There's a part of me that won't..." I find it useful to use that self-description as a way of explaining how the process of changing out of the smoking habit works

## All Parts of You Want What's Best for You

As strange as this seems, there is no part of you that is trying to do you in. All parts of you have good intentions, even that part that keeps you using tobacco products. They are simply attempting to satisfy your needs. The problem comes with the behaviors that some of those parts adapt to satisfy those needs. This is a very important distinction because it takes the fight, that internal, infernal battle, out of the recovery equation. Once we have acknowledged that the part keeps us using has only the best intention for us, we can start an internal conversation where we can thank that part for its concern and intention, and then suggest that it might help us explore other ways of satisfying those intentions -- the ones that also allow the other parts whose intentions are to keep the body healthy, wealthy and well -- to be able to support the new behavior.

The way the internal dialog or conversation would go is something like this: "Thank you very much for your wanting the best for me. Right now, I am working on other ways of satisfying those needs you are so concerned about. So, for the time being, I would love your support in my explorations for more effective and healthier ways of caring out your good intentions. I welcome your feedback as we try out these new ways. I only ask you to give these new ways a good trial run before judging their effectiveness. I am told that six months would be a fair trial period. I know that since you have my best interests in mind that you will be totally on board to explore even better ways of getting your intentions met then that of smoking. Thank you... Now where was I?"

That last question, "Thank you...Now where was I?" will bring you back to what you were doing before the thought of having a smoke, vape, or chew entered your mind. This conversation is an important one to have both before starting a tobacco-free lifestyle and regularly during the initial stages of the withdrawal process. Another way of saying that is "what you resist persists." The best way to stop negative thoughts is to acknowledge them and then get back to the new thinking. That is what that internal conversation accomplishes.

This all might sound silly at first until we realize that we regularly talk to ourselves. Unfortunately, most of that talk is negative, especially when it comes to ceasing bad habits. There are a lot of positive payoffs or benefits that are derived from bad habits so the part that controls that habit will fiercely fight for the habit to continue until it understands that the habit is no longer needed to provide the benefits.

In the case of smoking, there are a lot of payoffs or benefits – nicotine is a stimulant; the second most active ingredient, acetaldehyde, is a calming agent; the smoke, itself provides a literal "smoke screen to ease social discomfort; and the physical act of smoking, the moving of the cigarette to the mouth and back down again and again, gives the hands something to do when doing nothing with the hands is socially uncomfortable.

This process of acknowledging the intention of the controlling part of the mind, and enlisting its cooperation in exploring new methods and behaviors to still achieve the payoffs that the old habit provided, is a great technique because it utilizes the internal conversation that most people already use to explain why they are defeated from achieving their goals by their own mind and turns it into a positive force for change.

Some people find it quite helpful to have a coach to talk to as they go through this process. The inner mind work is much easier to do with a counselor or coach to guide you through. With stopping the smoking addiction, it would help to choose a coach who has successfully stopped for a long period of time and who is coaching from having walked the walk rather than from someone who coaching from formula and can only talk the talk. Specifically, for smoking cessation, finding a coach who is also well versed in hypnotherapy and/or NLP would probably be the best bet.

JASON WITTMAN, MPS, LAADC, CATC-IV

**What you imagine, you realize, so, daily visualize a new tobacco-free life.**

Once you are in a relaxed state, you can then run a little mental movie in which you visualize how you are now living a smoke-free life. For each scenario where you used to use tobacco products, picture and imagine yourself easily, confidently, and happily doing that activity tobacco-free and notice how great it feels to be able to breathe freely again. Notice how much money you are now able to save or whatever are the reasons why you decided to become tobacco-free. The important ingredient of this visualization is that it needs to be done in the present tense, i.e.: "I am having......" rather than, "I will have......" The inner mind does not distinguish past from future and only operates in the now, so, even though it seems like a strange construction, say, "The next time I am in a social situation, I am totally at ease..." It works the best.

# A GENTLE REMINDER

Scan this QR Code for a special and personal message from Jason.
And a bonus, 45 page "deep-dive" eBook

Or go to:
http://wittmanent.groovepages.com/offer

# SECTION III

## Intentionally create a joyous life

*"The art of living lies less in eliminating our troubles than growing with them."*
*~ attributed to Bernard M. Baruch*

The remainder of this book will cover how to successfully and exquisitely navigate that sometimes battlefield and mostly glorious adventure called living life. The philosopher, Chuang Tzu wrote that when the shoe fits, the foot is forgotten. We are only aware of the foot when it is in pain from an ill-fitting shoe. Much of life is that way. When things are going just hunky-dory, there is little or no conscious realization of the happenings of that moment and our part in it. We are just unconsciously participating. Unless we purposefully pay attention to life, the actors in it and our surroundings, we will blithefully blunder along until "the shoe" in the form of a current happening doesn't fit. Then we are jolted into that uncomfortable reality without a clear understanding of how it happened.

My intention is to provide the knowledge, awareness and skills to do life with eyes wide open and the ability to be able to anticipate when the shoe might not fit too well, to make the necessary mid-course corrections and intentionally create a mostly smooth-sailing, joyous life.

## The Map is Not the Territory

> "Is your life story the truth? Yes, the chronological events are true. Is it the whole truth? No. You see and judge it through your conditioned eyes and mind - not of all involved - nor do you see the entire overview. Is it nothing but the truth? No, you select, share, delete, distort, subtract, assume and add what you want, need and choose to."
>
> ~ Rasheed Ogunlaru

Our perceptions of our world are just that, perceptions, the way we see or visualize it. That perception may or may not be an accurate description of the actual reality. Part of exquisitely navigating life's territories is to be constantly questioning

JASON WITTMAN, MPS, LAADC, CATC-IV

whether our beliefs are based on the actual territories or our assumptions of them. Some of the basic territories that we exist in are a network of environments. The following descriptions of the environments in which we live is so that, with an awareness of their existence, there will be less confusion between the territories (the actual environments in which we live) and the maps (our beliefs of what they should be, not what they are.)

After that, I will present my prescriptions on how to best navigate both our internal and external worlds. The NLP 101 section will describe state of the art methods of communicating to oneself and to others. The Inside Stuff section includes some of my basic prescriptions for setting us up internally to win. And then the Relationships 101 section is a deep dive into the Relationships Environment and the makings of a near perfect relationship. The final section is on Writing for Your Life where I will teach you the secrets of near automatic self-expression.

# The Environment Always Wins!

*~To Be Aware Is To Be Alive~*

The study of our environments is critical to creating a successful life. Sure, much of successful outcomes in life have to do with the work and effort that we put into accomplishing them. Those efforts can be undone by paying little or no attention to our environments. The more we are aware of our environments and to what degree they are or are not supportive, the more we can assure that outcomes will be positive and permanent.

## Internal Environment

### Inner Environment

The Inner environment is the first and most important of the environment in which we live. It is the inner mind one, our thinking process including the way we think about ourselves, our self-esteem and self-confidence. We get clues about this by listening to our self-talk. Do we have a "can do" or a "no can do" approach to how we walk through the challenges of living?

There is an interesting online discussion that Tony Robbins had with two other multi-millionaire self-help gurus that focused directly on this environment. They were discussing a phenomenon that they had regularly observed. A good percentage of the people who buy their fairly high priced, self-help DVD courses, never even open the box. Tony offered an explanation that I am sure is correct. He said that their inner environment, aka their inner mind programming tells them that it does not matter what they try to do, they are losers and it won't work. What happens is that they get very enthused by the sales

JASON WITTMAN, MPS, LAADC, CATC-IV

pitch but by the time the program arrives, their old programming and its self-talk mantra of "It ain't going to work, so why bother!" is in full swing and the goes in the closet alongside all the variety of other self-help programs and devices, like muscle building machines, they bought and never used.

There are many ways to change negative inner environmental programs; hypnotherapy, Neuro-Linguistic Programming (NLP), self-hypnosis, repetition while acting "as if," and working with a coach who is skilled at walking clients through this reawakening process. All of them work to varying degrees and speed. The reason they work is due to the principle that the inner mind (aka, the unconscious) will automatically do whatever it understands is normal and natural. If the accumulated traumas and disappointments of an unsuccessful life have it understanding that losing is normal and natural, it will support negative thinking. The good news is that using those methods, listed above, the inner mind can become convinced that winning is normal and natural and when that happens, it will produce behaviors that are conducive to winning.

Hypnotherapists have known this for ages. We say, "What the inner mind imagines, it tends to realize." This is the gist of "The Secret." It has never been a secret to us. I just saved you some good money. You don't have to buy the movie or the book, now. Put that money to better use and invest in a good self-hypnosis, self-esteem program or if your inner thinking is very negative, the services of a good hypnotherapist, a practitioner of neuro-linguistic programming, or a life coach (or me who is trained in all the above) who can teach you this stuff and coach you through it. Once the inner mind environment becomes supportive of your goals, everything is possible.

## The Information Environment

The second is the information environment. This is a very important one. This environment encompasses all the information to which we are regularly exposed. All of the media, all our online browsing, including the endless memes, the cultural messages we grew up with, the newspapers we read, the TV shows and movies we watch, the advertising we see, read and hear, the books we read, all influence the way we perceive our world. The more we are exposed to the same messages the more they permeate into what our inner mind recognizes as being normal and natural. When that happens, it becomes part of our belief system and when that happens, we will operate off of those beliefs without question, even when, if we ever did question them, we would realize how they were negatively affecting our behavioral choices. In my world we call those beliefs, "limiting beliefs," and in the 12-Step world, "character defects."

As a counselor and mentor coach, much of what I do is assist my clients to explore their beliefs to uncover which of those are actually limiting beliefs. For most people, it really takes someone like me asking those, "Is that really going to achieve the outcomes you desire?" type of questions, for them to finally recognize their limiting beliefs.

"To be Aware is to be Alive!" As with all these environments we are exploring, the overriding reason to study them is to become aware of what they are and how much influence they can have on our lives. Once we are aware, we can protect ourselves from their negative influences. With information ones, we must set up filters to screen out negative informational inputs from everything we read, see and hear. Even without the assistance of a coach or a counselor it is possible to uncover many limiting beliefs by questioning how well the things we accept as the way things are, fit into our fundamental core belief system. We can also explore how well what we believe is congruent with what information we are exposing ourselves to.

JASON WITTMAN, MPS, LAADC, CATC-IV

## The Spiritual Environment

My definition of spiritual in this context is a bit broader than usual. I see it as that intangible construct that allows people to make sense out of the unexplainable and unanswerable parts of their lives and their worlds. For many people that is a belief in a higher power that can be labeled in many ways. Many people will find organized religious organization, churches, synagogues and mosques, that supports and helps strengthen that belief. For others who do not believe in ethereal, higher power explanations, including those who call themselves atheists, they have various ways of explaining the unexplainable that range from "the universe" to scientific theories.

It is very important to work on a personal unifying explanation of, as one author called it, "Why bad things happen to good people." Without some sort of a spiritual grounding, a person can risk falling into a downward, depressive cycle as a result of unexplainable personal trauma and tragedy. Having the ability to call on the comfort of feeling like they are not alone in the world has assisted lots of people get through troubled times.

For this environment, we need to inventory what we believe to be our version of a spiritual force. How do we nurture that belief? Do we pray, meditate, write, or use other ritualized practices to connect with that force? Are we supported by a community of like-minded people? Do our spiritual concepts support our ability to be at peace with our lives? Is there anything that is getting in the way of our having a firm connection with that spiritual belief? If so, are we doing anything to change or are we just tolerating it and living in resentments?

If you are having problems in this area, it can be really useful to work with a professional who can explore the above questions so that they will be able assist you to fine tune your sense of spirituality. Doing that, you will have the comfort of knowing that you are supported in your journey through them, regardless of the circumstances you find yourself in.

## The Personal Self Environment

So far in our explorations of the Environments we have looked at the inner mind, the information, and the spiritual ones. And now, the personal self-environment. This one encompasses all the non-physical attributes of a person, such as personality, strengths and vulnerabilities, and talents.

I find that many of the clients that I work with, especially those who are working on enhancing their self-confidence and self-esteem have never taken the time to accurately inventory all these qualities that make them who they are. There are a lot of limiting beliefs that are associated with a person's self-concept. Many of them come from early childhood where they were teased or harassed about their physical attributes such as their height or lack thereof. It is not until they finally take as unbiased a look at themselves as a whole do can they stare to see where maybe they bought into someone else's stupid, uninformed biases.

A good example of this is from my own experience. When I was in ROTC summer camp, I was walking down the hall in the barracks wearing short pants. Another cadet approached me and as he was walking by, commented that if he had knees like mine, he would never wear shorts. From that day until not very long ago, when, with hugely more self-esteem, I questioned my 45-year-old clothing decision, I did not wear shorts. By the way, I didn't know nor did I ever see that cadet again. Because my self-esteem was quite low at that time, a random stranger's single comment was adopted as fact.

The first mission is to make a list of all the unique talents and strengths that you know you have. Look at your skills, your innate abilities, the qualities of you that others admire and love (if you don't know, then ask the people closest to you what they admire and love about you). Only when you notice and accept all those attributes that make you the wonderful you that you are, can you fully develop a great self-concept.

As with all these environments, it is important to become aware of what you are tolerating in your personal self-environment. Are there traits that you have that you know are impeding your ability to reach your goals that you are putting up with rather than dealing with them? An example of that might be the habit of never letting others finish what they are saying before you respond which is losing you valuable associates.

When you have thoroughly explored this environment you ought to be able to have a good idea of who you are, know that you are worthy of other people's love and support and have a good feeling of your potential to succeed in your life.

## The Personal Financial Environment

This environment includes money, budgeting, investments, earnings, spending and our relationship to the acquisition of wealth.

One of the most important parts of the environment has to be our relationship to the acquisition of money. By that I mean, how we value our time and service as well as our attitudes towards acquiring wealth. Is it OK for us culturally to be wealthy? Like most inner mind things, if the answer to this one is that "I am unworthy of having more money" then I will lack that motivation to aggressively pursue money by not asking for raises or not raising prices and pricing my products and services below market value.

Other strong influences in this environment are budgeting and investment planning and a good accounting system. Without these in place or with a slipshod system, the chance of acquiring wealth to retire on is slim. In the short run, lack of financial management will increase the chances of short run financial drama in the form of late charges on credit cards, higher interests due to late payments and lots of calls we would rather not have.

As with all the environments, it is very good to question what if anything we are tolerating in relation to financial matters. Are we putting up with being paid less than we feel we are worth? Are we working for the money or do we really love our occupations?

There is an old saying, "Money does not bring you happiness, but it sure can make happiness more comfortable!" Paying attention to our financial environment will go a long way towards ensuring a comfortably happy life.

## External Environments

### The Personal Physical Environment

This is the immediate environment we live in, the apartment, the house and its yard as well as the inside of these dwellings. Because this is literally where we live, how we organize and decorate that living space hugely influences our lives. The Chinese recognized the importance of this to the degree that they developed a technology called Feng shui to optimize the effectiveness of one's living space.

There are many things that contribute to how supportive a living environment is. Is it well-lit either with good lighting or plenty of windows? What colors are the walls? Is there a lot of clutter? Is it a comfortable and embarrassment-free place to entertain guests? If cooking is a desired activity, does it have a well-functioning kitchen?

Hopefully you get the idea. Next to the Inner Environment, this one is of almost equal importance because this one immediately supports your lifestyle. A dark, drearily painted and cluttered living space will be depressing to even the most well motivated people.

## The Personal Relationship Environment

It is time to get really personal in this exploration of our environments. This is all about family, close friends and colleagues. This one is not only personal; it is quite critical to growth and success. The mantra of "The Environment Always Wins!" is especially true when it comes to relationships. The clichés of "You are as good as the company you keep" and a quaint country version of it, "If you sleep with pigs, you end up smelling like pig shit!" are based on a millennium of painful experiences as a result of poor relationship choices.

Some of the ways that relationships can contribute to personal disaster include; the naysayers, negative people, and people with different aspirations and life direction than yours. If you are a creative person, an innovator, or an entrepreneur, the worst people to hang out with or ask for an opinion about your latest creation or project are the naysayers. They will tell you every way it isn't going to work. Many times, they will do it with very good intentions of being the "devil's advocate." That's a great service to call upon prior to the launch of a project, as a final bug check, but during the creative process, that kind of negative support can be disastrous.

Living or working in an environment filled with negative folks, such as depressed people and people with no drive or enthusiasm for life will eventually take its toll on even those with the most positive attitudes. Likewise, living with people whose life goals are fundamentally different from your aspirations, can make getting to your goals way more of a project than it need be. For example, I once had a client who was in the process of starting a new business and was living in a retirement community. With most of his friends retired or actively planning retirement, the topics of most conversations were about their next cruise or golf game and they had very little interest in discussions of his latest business venture. Eventually he found that he was losing focus on his new venture, in favor of thinking about the next game of golf. When he joined a small business organization and joined their social activities, his focus and enthusiasm for his project soared.

Hopefully, you have an appreciation for how important being aware of who is in your relationship environment and to what degree they are supportive of continuing self-development. Part of that awareness needs to be the awareness of who, amongst your relationships, you are tolerating and what is the cost of tolerating them in your life. As with all tolerations, it is important to weigh the positive payoffs of keeping the source of the toleration around vs. the negatives including building resentments for that source. You might have a spouse or relative that is a naysayer and yet is a powerfully positive loving part of your life. Once aware of that negative aspect, you could find other folks to bounce new ideas off of. No one person needs to fulfill all needs in your life. The best way of dealing with tolerations is to get rid of the source or, in this case, recognize that they are who they are and go find other people who are better fitted for the task.

For people who are in recovery from alcohol, drugs and other non-chemical addictions, it is ultra-important to pay close attention to these close-in environments. Especially in early recovery, the environment literally, always wins! People spend months in the positive rehab environments and then think that they can return to the neighborhood and friends they had when they were in their active addictions. Initially, they will most probably be able to continue their recovery, but eventually the environment will get to them when all their close-in support is not only negative but aggressively interested in supporting their own limiting beliefs that recovery does not work by assisting them to fail.

JASON WITTMAN, MPS, LAADC, CATC-IV

## The Network Environment

Thank you for sticking with me this far. I hope by now you are getting a greater awareness of the environmental influences on your life and a greater appreciation for how great an influence they have on our life choices and attitudes.

The Network Environment consists of your customers or clients, your social networks both online and in person, your memberships in organizations and your partners and alliances.

Some of the considerations to ponder when evaluating how well your network environment is supporting your life and your goals include how well your network responds to your requests for help and assistance. Is the support one sided or do you and your network share referrals and information regularly? For networks to really work there needs to be a good degree of mutuality otherwise one side will feel sucked upon and resentments will grow and destroy the network relationship.

Whereas the personal environment will tend to have people who reflect your thinking, attitudes and lifestyle, the network environment, if cultivated well, is the place to be exposed to interesting and diverse opinions, cultures, experiences and backgrounds. A great network environment will serve as both a supportive one for your businesses and, with the exposure to new ideas, cultures, outlooks and novel ways of doing things, can be a catalyst for personal growth.

An important and often overlooked part of this environment is that of your clients and customers. Are these folks the ones that you like to work with, that inspire you to do your best work or are they people you dread to deal with or bore you to death? If it is the later, your business life will be a chore rather than a joy that you look forward to. Michael Port, in his great book, "Book Yourself Solid," introduced the concept of having a "red rope policy." Just like in the nightclub, where the Red Rope keeps the boring people out of that environment, having one for your business where you screen out or refer out clients you would rather not deal with, will greatly increase your level of enthusiasm where you look forward to going to work.

That was another way of asking if you are tolerating people in this environment. The fewer the tolerations, the more supportive this environment will be in your life.

## Neighborhood Environment

No matter where we are living, there will always be other things and people that will surround us. As with all the environments the neighborhood environment will eventually win. For recovering folks, if they return to their hood where they drank and used drugs, the chances of them staying clean and sober will be greatly diminished. If your community is not reflective of the life you would like to be living, then it behooves you to either change locations or if that is circumstantially impossible, once you leave your living space, quickly go hang out in a more supportive neighborhood.

## The Community Environment

Surrounding the neighborhood is the greater community and surrounding that is the city, town or village. Each one of these contributes to your living environment. The larger the geographic entity, the more of a general influence it will have on your environment.

The difference between the neighborhood and the community is that the neighborhood is the very local area surrounding your living space, the block and the surrounding blocks, whereas the community will be comprised of a bunch of smaller neighborhoods. It is very important to be aware of how each of these geographical entities is contributing to your external environment. On my

JASON WITTMAN, MPS, LAADC, CATC-IV

block in my immediate neighborhood, many of my neighbors will have weekend outdoor parties that may even include a band, but always includes loud music. For this reason, no one objects to me banging on my drums or having a group of folks jamming in my living room. In my last neighborhood, that was ethnically quieter, they would call the sheriff when we got too loud.

The purpose of calling attention to all these environments is so that we become very aware of how each of them has both direct and indirect influence on our wellbeing, our attitudes and our lives. If things don't seem to be going the way we would like, it is well worthwhile to examine if there is a negative contributing factor being exerted by one of the environments.

## The Greater World Environment

This environment encompasses the rest of the world that wraps around the immediate environments that we just explored. Beyond our communities are the cities, counties, states, and countries. Depending on their ethnic and social compositions, laws, social attitudes, tolerances or differences from the norm, etc., they will have varying degrees of influence over the daily lives of their inhabitants. Life can be made a lot easier if one was to choose to settle in a geographic area that was attuned to that person's, ethnicity, religious beliefs (or lack thereof), sexual and political identities. This is the reason why many folks self-ghettoize. Although making sure that all the previously discussed environments were working well in one's life would produce a comfortable life regardless of where in the greater world they were living, there could still be a great deal of discomfort if that greater world was antagonistic to one's lifestyle.

Being aware, is to be alive! Being aware of all these environments and how they are affecting you will allow for being able to consciously know just why "things are a bit uncomfortable, allowing for mid-course correction. We can become closer to actually seeing the territory instead of relying on a perceptual map.

# Prescriptions for Navigating Our Internal and External Worlds

## Neuro-Linguistic Programming (NLP) 101

A very important principle of Neuro-Linguistic Programming (NLP) is: "The content of a communication is in how it is received," In plain English, no matter what you intended, how it was taken or interpreted by the person who received it is what rules. That means the burden of presenting an unambiguous meaning is the 100% responsibility of the presenter. For this reason, learning the skills of neuro-linguistic programming, allows you to be spontaneous in a way that actually communicates your spontaneity exactly as you intended it. It also gives you the ability to quickly know when your intention is being misunderstood.

Neuro-linguistic programming was developed by one of my earliest mentors, John Grinder, Ph.D., and his collaborators as a way of giving communicators the tools to replicate the most effective techniques of the most effective communicators. They studied some of the most effective communicators with the purpose of figuring out just what they did to be so effective. They looked at everything; the way their model communicators spoke, the words they used, the tone, the speed, etc., and then used what the team had observed as a model to see if they could achieve the same results. They also observed everyday folk in their conversations with others to see if there were things that were unconsciously being done that put the people either in or out of rapport. Being trained as linguists, they also paid attention to the words that people used as well as any physical clues that related to their choice of words and meanings.

Here is a short course and introduction to the art of Neuro-Linguistic Programming (NLP). Any and everything I am about to describe can and ought to be verified by your own observations. I intentionally used "ought to" because unless you observe these things and try out the techniques for yourself, they will remain just facts instead of becoming useful communications tools.

## Representational Systems

People primarily process information, think and speak in one of three representational systems; visual, auditory (sound) and kinesthetic (touch, feel, physical sensations.) It is important to know these systems and their use in both yourself and others. If there is a mismatch between speaker and listener, there is a good chance that not only will the message be less understood, but it might not be heard at all. Each of these systems is like speaking a different language or, at the least, a strange dialect of a language. A Londoner speaking to a person speaking with a very intense Scottish accent would know they are speaking English and would understand little of what is being expressed.

### Format of representational systems

For each of these systems, the description will follow the format of:

1. The general internal process,
2. How that is presented in the words and phrases that are spoken, and, as it was discovered,
3. From eye movements, clues both to the system they are operating in. For some reason, our brains are wired up to our eyes in such a way that depending on which representational system we are accessing, the eyes will move in very specific ways. For visual thoughts, the eyes move upward. Auditory thoughts - level with the ground. Kinesthetic (Feeling) thoughts and when having internal conversations - looking down, and;

4. if the thought expressed was from a memory or it was just thought up and a newly constructed one. Looking to the right or left will indicate if the thoughts are remembered ones or newly constructed ones. Which way an individual moves their eyes (left or right) will vary from person to person so that will be determined by observing the direction as they talk about either a memory or a new thought. Once this is determined for an individual, it will apply to them forever.

**One last caveat:** What follows are the primary systems that operate in individuals. The other two are usually also present, though relegated to minor roles and appearances although in certain situations might temporarily become dominant. It is therefore important to observe over time and check out your conclusions with more observations to figure out the dominant system. This process in NLP terms is called "calibrating." The nice thing is that once that is done, there is a greater certainty of reliability and still it is important to regularly calibrate, for those temporary changes.

**Visual System**

1. The internal thinking process will most likely be a visual one. Even where the thought is about something that was said or will be said, the thought will first be a picture of the sayer, rather than the actual sound of the words said.
2. A visual person will speak in visual words and terms. For example, words such as *see, look, observe, view, and appear,* and in phrases such as *mental image, mind's eye clear-cut, and point out.* Some visual phrases literally make no sense at all, such as *"I can see what you are saying."*
3. Eye movements: Eyes will be looking up when accessing visual thoughts.
4. Tempo and volume of speech: Visual people tend to talk loud and fast

**Auditory System**

1. The internal process for auditory people is via sound. They think, internally file things and talk in sound terms.
2. Auditory folks predominantly use auditory words and phrases: Words such as: *say, mention, divulge, earshot, quiet, utter, and remark* and phrases such as; *clear as a bell, to tell the truth, loud and clear, and crystal clear.*
3. Auditory thoughts will be accessed when the eyes are parallel to the ground.
4. Auditory people will talk quieter and slower and more rhythmically than visual ones.

**Kinesthetic (feeling) System**

1. Accessing feelings and also when people have internal conversations (talk to themselves) requires looking down. The direction they are looking (r or l) while they are looking down will determine whether they are accessing feelings or having internal conversations. It will be different for different people, so it has to be calibrated. (Right-handed people will usually have the opposite direction from left-handed ones.)
2. The words kinesthetic folks will use are generally tactile or feeling ones such as *grasp, grip, unbearable, stressed, anxious, feel, and warm.* Phrases include; *Get a handle on, hold on, pain-in-the-neck, cool calm, and collected, can't get a grasp, and floating on air.*
3. Kinesthetic people will talk excessively slowly and seemingly engaged in thought.

## The Art of Establishing Rapport

Using this new learning, let's apply it along with some other effective techniques to the art of establishing rapport. The dictionary defines rapport as "a close and harmonious relationship in which people or groups feel "in sync" with each other, understand each other's feelings or ideas and communicate smoothly." The NLP founders observed people in conversation, who obviously fit that definition. They noticed a number of characteristics, the more of which were present, were good predictors of how solid the rapport was. They noticed that the participants mirrored each other in every way from tone and pace of their speech to their physiology. They also noticed that one of the best matches was that of representational systems.

You can verify this finding for yourself if you are to wander into a coffee shop where couples are in deep conversation. Notice that they are unconsciously matching each other's physiology. If one has his legs crossed so will the other. The same for leaning on an elbow. Even down to if one rubs his eyes, the chances are that the other will quite soon make a similar motion. If you could get close enough to overhear the conversation, you would probably observe matches in tone, volume, cadence, and other nuances of speech. The takeaway is that the more one can match the other person, the better that the other person is going to feel that there is a harmonious match. There is little chance of the other person thinking you are doing a Simon Says routine with them because they will not be aware of what they are doing but matching those things will unconsciously add to the feelings of rapport. All of this is important to establish rapport and the most important one that will clinch the deal is matching representational systems.

Now let's say that you were attempting to establish good rapport with someone. As suggested, you mirrored them by matching their speech rhythms, their primary representational system, their physiology (what they were doing with their body; crossing feet, slouching, sitting straight, etc.). In neuro-linguistic programming terms that is called pacing. The question is, is there a test for knowing if all this is working? The answer is yes. The easiest way is when you feel that there is some good rapport happening, alter something in your physiology, uncross your feet, lean on an elbow if your hands were in your lap, or switch to leaning on the other elbow. If in 20 - 30 seconds, the other person also makes that switch so that your physiologies would be matched, that would not only verify rapport but also, at an unconscious level, establish your recognized lead. If the other person does not follow your shift, they go back to pacing (imitating) them for a while and keep testing until you get a positive response.

It is useful to think of these systems as if they were separate languages. Which presents a problem when we are attempting to speak to someone who processes information in a different system unless we are able to detect a mismatch and be flexible enough to speak in their system. Here is an example of translating into another system:

- Statement: "My past is clouded"
  - o   Visual match: I can't see much of my past.
  - o   Auditory: I can't tune into my past.
  - o   Kinesthetic: I can't get a grasp of my past.
- Statement: Jim gets fired up at exam time.
  - o   Kinesthetic match: Jim gets excited at exam time.
  - o   Visual: Jim looks forward to exams.
  - o   Auditory: Jim is in a shouting good mood at exam time.

Corny, but you get the point.

## Strategies

Strategies, in this context, are a study of the mental process that a person goes through as they decide to do, think or feel anything. Most decisions we make are thought of as being one step but actually, they are the summation of many micro-decisions or processes that involve the utilization of all of the representational systems. Although especially in sales but also in all intrapersonal communications it is very useful to know a person's strategies.

In sales, it is very useful to know that the process your customer uses to get to a buying decision is to: 1. Visually check out the item. 2. Check out their feelings about that visual image. 3. Auditorily, ask a friend's opinion 4. Compare how the friend's opinion compares to their feelings. 5. Physically interact with the item and evaluate their reaction to it physically, i.e.: try on the jacket or sit on the chair. 6. Maybe get more opinions from others, and then 7. Make a buying decision. And possibly 8. Questioning the wisdom of that decision (buyer's remorse.)

Why is knowing this important? A real-life example: my buying strategy is 1. Check out visually and then, and only then, check out the feel, comfort, etc. If I am in a clothing store and encounter a salesperson who attempts to get me to try on every jacket I look at and doesn't get the hint that visually appealing to me is my number one priority, I will either leave the store or actually tell them to stay away from me until I call for them. I once had a salesman who understood my strategy and suggested that before I start looking, we just try on random jackets for size and fit only, and then he would point me to the section where I could make my choices. He retreated until I picked the most likely candidates and then he went to work laying out combinations of outfits for me. Before him, I had walked out of three other stores. With him, I walked out with more than a thousand dollars of clothes.

## Anchoring

Just like an anchor ties a boat to the ocean floor, our lives utilize all sorts of anchors to tie our feelings, memories, and reactions to former occurrences, experiences or actions. Anchors can be via any of the five senses; sight, sound, touch, taste, or smell. "They are playing our song!" is an auditory anchor that ties to the warm, fuzzies of when we met. Of all the discoveries of NLP, anchors are one of the most useful to understand and master.

Some of the general characteristics and rules of anchors:

1. An anchor will get tied to the strongest feeling or experience. For example, birthday cakes are usually a visual anchor to happy, fun occasions but if an earthquake struck in the middle of a birthday celebration, cakes from then on could end up as an anchor to feelings of terror and disaster.
2. An anchor can be set with one occurrence although repeated similar occurrences or experiences that are tied to the same anchor will reinforce that association. NLP calls that "Stacking Anchors."
3. Although anchors are usually one of the five senses, they can also be a thought or remembrance of one of those senses. I could be thinking about chocolate cake and get terror feelings of that earthquake.
4. Triggers are the sensory stimulus that will set off the remembrance of the feelings, etc. that it was anchored to. Knowing this about anchors, it is important to make sure that we do not inadvertently set an anchor in a negative way. See the Love Strategies section for powerful examples of this principle.
5. Anchors are very specific. Different smells can anchor very different experiences as can different touches or hugs.

## Communicate precisely and fully

Choose your words well. Synonyms are not all equal in their actual, emotional, and, even more important, meta (the underlying message beneath the message) meanings. Some examples: "should" has a value judgment attached to it, whereas, "could" just indicates a choice. And "could," itself, can mean different things depending on who is speaking it. "When you get a chance, could you please......" means very different things when coming from a friend a request) vs. from your boss (a friendly way of giving an order). If you happen to be the boss of your friend, don't be surprised or angry if your friendly order is interpreted as a request.

It is also prudent to be aware of psycho-semantic words. "Psycho-semantics is a word I have coined to describe the study of words in the English language whose intended meaning is quite different from its dictionary definition. They are words that sometimes are emotionally loaded, such as "should vs. could." They also are words like "try" which is used as a synonym of "attempt" but invariably means an attempt that the speaker unconsciously believes will fail. How many times has someone told you, "I will try to call you"? Don't hold your breath. If they really wanted to call, they would have said, "Let's talk next Wednesday at 3 PM."

There is an old saying "To ass-u-me is to make an ass of you and me." Unless we, speakers, are crystal clear that everyone in the conversation is operating from the same set of assumptions, it is imperative to assume nothing!

When I was in a driver's education class, a very, very long time ago, one of my classmates, Jean, nearly failed her driving exam when the tester did not make his direction clear and assumed she would understand. She asked the tester, as they approached an intersection, "Should I continue straight ahead:" He answered, "Right." She understood "right" to mean O.K. and proceeded to drive into a dead end. The tester meant "turn right" and was furious at her. Fortunately for her, after he verbally blew up at her, he realized that it was his mistake for assuming, apologized, and passed her.

### Elicit Feedback

You must check to make sure that what you said is what was heard. If you can't figure this out from the listener's response, it is then your obligation to ask questions to make sure they got it. "Do you understand?" is a terrible feedback question because a "yes" reply does not give you a clue as to "what" they understand. All you know is that they understand something. A better question might be, "Exactly what did you get from my explanation?" or better yet, ask a question that calls for the information you just delivered to be used to formulate the answer, such as: "How do you think you could use this method to calm out of control children?" If you use clear, precise language and explanations and elicit feedback to check how your message was received, you will have gone a long way towards developing yourself as an effective communicator.

## Universal Quantifiers

Universal Quantifiers are adjectives that when used will have the effect of limiting choices when it comes to describing personal situations or when used in arguments, attempting to win by sneaking in an absolute. The adjectives are "never," "all," "nothing," "never," "always," 'every." They are referred to as "universal" because when used, they leave zero room for any other occurrence than the thought with which they are associated.

When they are used by you to describe a situation you are in, they serve the purpose of keeping you stuck in the status quo because they leave no room for anything other than the current situation. For instance, "I never seem to get an even break!" totally ignores the times when things really worked out quite well.

The best way of dealing with universal quantifiers when they come up in personal thoughts or in conversations with others is by taking the quantifier and asking it as a question. Never? Always? All? Another effective counter to them is to ask for exceptions such as, "Were their times when you DID win?" or "Can you remember a time when it did rain in Los Angeles?"

As with all things NLP where the content of a communication is in how it is received by the listener. Preciseness counts! Using universal quantifiers is hardly ever accurate because few things in the world are monolithic. When we use it in self-talk, we are probably lying to ourselves or participating in high drama. When used with others, it is usually a lie, even when it is an unconscious one. So, I, for one, always make it a practice to never use every one of these in all my communications with both no one and everyone.

## Inside Stuff

This section includes some of my basic prescriptions for setting up your insides to win so that you will actually do what you intended to do. True confession: not everything in this section will be logically related to everything else. Throughout this book, I have made an effort to create a logical, topical flow. This section is just a catch-all one where I am putting all those prescriptions that I know are important, though do not seem to fit in a particular place.

### Getting Out of The Way

*~ The Way Waits for Eyes Unclouded by Longing! ~ Ram Das*

One day when I was taking a shower, I just let my voice go where it wanted to go and it came out with one of the most perfectly lovely of melodies, totally freeform and inventive. There was not one note that was out of place or off-key. It was just beautiful. This got me thinking that this is a perfect example of getting out of the way.

Everything of beauty, every bit of true thought, all of the creative energies of the human potential are unleashed when one gets out of the way. In performance and in sports this is labeled "Being in the zone. The question is how does one create an ability to get out of the way, at will? There are many ways of cultivating that ability. The spiritual understanding is there is a God-force or for those uncomfortable with the "G" word, a "greater source of wisdom and knowledge." If that force is allowed to flow through our inner mind and out through the mouth or the fingers or the body action, it will produce perfect thought and action. Of course, there is no proof that such a source exists. It is a very useful construct though. The mind works well when fed such useful constructs. The real question, though, is once that construct is adopted, how does one go about doing it. Just how do you "get out of the way?"

A more basic question might be, just what has to be gotten out of the way to allow this pure thought and action to flow? The "what" is the outer or conscious mind. When it is out of the way, the "what" that gets to use that pure thought and action is the inner or unconscious mind. The inner mind is in charge of all those things that we do automatically. It keeps us from bumping into things when we are walking and not consciously paying attention. It keeps us in the lane and guides us around road hazards that suddenly appear in front of us on the freeway, long before the outer mind realizes they're there. Incidentally, that is a good example of a situation where the outer mind is out of the way and the inner mind delivers. I have been in near-accidents at high speeds on California's freeways and what made them "near" accidents, instead of catastrophes was that my inner mind did what it needed to do to guide my hands to steer through the chaos. My outer mind caught up to what had just happened, miles later!

In the realm of mind things, the outer mind is a minor player and mostly is a performance inhibitor. It is the part that says, "What should I do next?" and "If I was to do that, what would people say?" It also provides bits of useful information like reminding us that the next freeway exit is ours and that our fly is unzipped. It also can be a huge negative player when it is questioning one's abilities and especially when it wants to direct what needs to be an unconscious process. A good example is the process of learning an instrument or learning to type. The outer mind wants to make sure that it is being done right, so it takes charge of where the fingers should be placed. The problem is that the outer mind will never be able to think fast enough for the fingers to be able to achieve proficiency. Proficiency can only happen when it is directed by the inner mind. Comparing the computational speeds of the outer mind vs. the inner mind would be like comparing half the speed of sound to four times the speed of light. That is why the outer mind needs to get out of the Way.

So how can one purposefully learn to get out of the way? Here are some of the ways I do it:

1.  Someone in New York City once asked for directions to Carnegie Hall, one of the major concert venues of the time, by asking, 'How do you get to Carnegie Hall? The answer he got back was, "Practice! Practice! Practice!" Although not too useful to find the place, it is quite useful to get to the point where the outer mind feels it can relinquish control and get totally out of the way and allow the musical abilities to flow out at a concert hall level of expertise. Whether it is playing an instrument, playing sports, doing crossword puzzles, singing, public speaking, writing, or acting, practicing to the point where the skill becomes an automatic unconscious process is an essential first step.

2.  Even with lots of practice and even after the skills are almost automatic, sometimes the expected expert performance does not happen. This is usually due to the outer mind getting in the way. If you ever learned to type you have had this experience. There is a point where your fingers know what keys to press to produce the right result but you are still looking at your fingers because you consciously want to make sure they really

know where to press. Once you resisted all temptation to look and type a passage flawlessly and repeat that a number of times, the outer mind will be convinced and stop monitoring. Only then will your typing speed make dramatic Increases.

3. There are times when the outer mind refuses to stop its monitoring and controlling functions and sometimes even produces negative behaviors to sabotage the whole effort. What can be done to get it to cooperate or to do an endplay around it? These problems are usually caused by "inner game" issues. There is some part of the inner personality that has serious reservations with the course of action that the person is undertaking and is slowing down or stopping the process in an effort to protect the person. My assumption when talking about this process is to understand that all actions of this nature by the inner personality are done with positive intention and never with malevolence. Unfortunately, sometimes the behaviors that are chosen to carry out that intention can be pretty lousy. So if you are doing everything you can with the first two suggestions and still come up with inner game impedances like anxiety, stage fright, procrastination, or a hesitancy to play full-out, the first course to deal with them would be to use the self-help techniques of creative visualization and self-hypnosis. If all the tools you have are not working, then it is probably time to call on the services of a professional to guide you through the process. Those professionals that are most qualified to do this are coaches and counselors who also have Neuro-Linguistic Programming and, even better, hypnotherapy skills. With that assistance, you will be on your way to mastery.

## Overcoming Writer's block by getting out of the way, a personal recollection.

I sometimes find that my writing hits a dead end. I am writing a piece and the thoughts just stop coming. The words are no longer flowing out of my mind as they normally would do. I am spending eons on each sentence. The creative world has stopped. The more I try to create, the worse it gets and the greater my level of frustrating becomes, until, as it happened to me a while ago, I ripped the pages I had just painstakingly written out of the Notebook crumbled them up, and throw them across the room! Then I remembered my own directions on how to win the writing game, "get out of the way!" I work best when I just put the pen to the paper and let the right side of my brain, the creative side inner mind, just do its work and put pure thought onto the page (as it is doing now as I am writing this). When I set up the conditions for that process to happen, I get great results.

What happened with my writing that day is a great case-in-point. Actually, what happened with my writing for the three prior days is the full case-in-point. I decided that my next blog would be an article on how to win the game of life. A great topic and one that I regularly coach people to do and write books about, like this one. The intro flowed out effortlessly. Then instead of just writing, I started to craft the article to make sure that everything was presented logically and succinctly. Each word and paragraph became harder and harder to write. It was as if I had started out on a walk on what was a level road and as I progressed down that road, some ethereal force kept raising the angle of the road until I was finally clawing my way up a cliff.

Well, it was not an ethereal force that raised the pitch of my writing road. It was that old destroyer of creative thought, the busy body left brain, the outer mind. The more I "tried" to get it correct, the worse it got, because the left brain, the outer mind, is the editor not the creator. The right brain, the inner mind, is

JASON WITTMAN, MPS, LAADC, CATC-IV

the creator. I had the process reversed. Editing as one is creating is a prescription for creative disaster.

As I ripped the pages out of the notebook and threw them across the room, I said, "What am I doing? I just destroyed three days of effort!" I then realized that in that last statement was the clue to the solution. The clue was the word "effort." Writing, and any creative process, when it is happening as a pure right grain, inner mind activity, is an "effortless" process. It just flows out.

My first impulse had been to retrieve the destroyed pages and try to resurrect my work but this new bit of enlightenment about "effortlessness" directed me to let that work go and get back to the basics which, in my case of creative writing, is to put the pen to the page and keep it moving and moving and moving until the right brain once again starts putting pure thought out onto the page. You are now reading the result of that action.

I have been talking about the writing process. This same prescription can apply to any creative endeavor. If you are a sculptor or a singer or a photographer or a creative whatever, the same prescription for getting out of a creative dead-end applies, STOP "TRYING" TO DO IT AND JUST DO IT!

Let's say you are a photographer. You can't seem to shoot a decent picture and your composition is out to lunch and you notice your level of frustration is getting out of sight and your output continues to drop. Stop what you are doing, take your camera and go for a walk. Pretend you are a wide-eyed child who is seeing the world for the very first time. Start taking pictures of it as fast as new scenes pop into view. Just shoot what you see; the bee on the flower, the ant dragging a bit of something bigger than itself, the cloud reflected in the mud puddle. Just keep shooting. Keep your attention on the subject in front of you and the next one and so on until you are around the block and back to the studio. Now go back to the project in which you were bogged down and shoot it as you have been shooting the subjects with the same spontaneous abandon as you were shooting the subjects on your creative walk. Be aware of when your left brain tries to get you back into the "proper" mechanics of photography, like composition and all that, and gently go back to just effortlessly shooting neat pictures. Notice the difference.

Creative stuff is supposed to be fun! When it stops being fun, you can bet that the left critical brain just took over. Lack of fun, decreasing productivity, and raising frustration are the clues to this happening. That is when you STOP efforting and go do your equivalent of the creative walk to get your right brain back in

the pilot's chair of your mind. We will revisit this in the writing section later on.

Postscript: I now have the destroyed notebook pages tacked on my office wall to remind me of this lesson.

## Chunking It On Down

This technique is how to successfully navigate through that seeming morass of "it's all too much". Even when we are playing full-out by coming from cause with 100% enthusiasm and commitment, there are times when the road ahead looks overwhelming. Like there is too much to do and too little time to do it.

There are two ways that a project can be viewed, globally or in chunks.

Global views are good to understand and grasp the entire concept or project. This view is great for long-range planning and mind mapping. While it is a great way to view the whole project, attempting to tackle a project from there can be both confusing and overwhelming.

For day-to-day planning the chunked on down view is preferable. By chunking it on down we break up the global view or thought into its component parts or bite-sized, easily handleable working units.

For example, let's say that there is a brick wall that needs to be demolished. Thinking of having to tackle that massive structure can be demoralizing and debilitating which can lead to procrastination and even abandonment of the mission. Rather than focusing on the entire wall, focusing on removing one brick at a time makes this project doable.

Only in the space called "today" can any constructive activity ever take place. Thinking about yesterday or tomorrow other than to quickly take stock of what has been done and what needs to be done to get where we want to go is time and energy that is no longer available to do today's footwork. Remember the past so as not to repeat the errors. Glance at the future to know what you are aiming for. But remember to dwell in the present, today, with one little chunk at a time. That's where all the work of a project gets done and, where one's life is accomplished.

The "today's footwork" is what moves projects ahead, including one's life work. This alone will influence how good an outcome is achieved at the end of that particular day.

In the Air Force, we had emphasized the 6Ps of every project. Previous Planning Prevents Piss Poor Performance. Preparing for the workflow and all the aspects of the project before starting is important, even though the advice is to avoid dwelling in the future.

Some of the tools to assist in that planning are readily available online.

- Mindmaps allow the elements of a project to be graphically presented and easily rearranged as your thinking changes. I have been using a mindmap as I have been writing this book. A way of thinking about mindmaps that it is a graphic presentation of chunks and sub-chunks.
- Microsoft's To Do program is an online list-building program. It is a place to build endless lists with the ability to set dates on items and check off when a task is accomplished. It is an app on the phone and on desktops and changing stuff on one immediately changes on all other copies.

Trello is the most useful free program I know of that keeps track of everything and in an orderly, easy to access presentation that allows for drag and drop rearranging of everything. It can be set up for individual projects or entire ongoing operations. I have used Trello to run a marketing agency. It allowed me to have individual files for every client and prospect with the ability to write a summary of every prospect, sales, and service conversation. You can download a free copy of Trello with this link: https://trello.com/jasonwittman/recommend

**The opposite of chunking it on down is Lumping it on up.**

Most people who are in the habit of negative, doom and gloom, thinking regularly do the opposite of chunking it on down. They are used to taking all those quite doable parts of a huge problem and lump them together into a massive undoable mess that defies a solution because all the elements of that mess are unrelated problems each of which has its own solution. Global Views are massively unproductive!

Recently a client of mind was moaning and groaning about how his current situation was a "total mess." We spent most of the session "chunking the situation on down" into all the elements that here-to-fore had been unsolved. We then problem solved each of these chunks and came up with doable solutions to either solve or constructively work around them. There was some noticeable relief as he acknowledged the progress we made and then came the "but,..." "But I don't know how I will ever get through this mess."

Out of habit, he had slipped back into the "lumping it on up" mantra, and from that "woe is me" position, it was impossible to recognize that we had just worked out solutions to all the elements, hence yanked right back into those depressing feeling he was feeling before we started the session. When I pointed out that he had just lumped on up all of those solved elements, and then quickly reviewed our multiple solutions he was able to once again focus on his doable solutions and was able to break out of that doom and gloom trance.

Lumping it on up is making an unsolvable mess out of very solvable parts.

## How Hypnotherapists get rid of Headaches without medicine

As I learned from the experiences of walking on red hot wood coals without ever getting even a small blister, our minds have much more ability to product positive physical results if unleashed to do so than we could ever image. For those of you who have never experienced this, it seems like a mystical fairytale. Having had the experience on three different occasions and then been on the Tony Robbins team that built and attended to the fires on many more events, I can attest that there is no magic or illusion involved. There is a learned skill of how to allow the mind to do its job to protect the body unencumbered by our limited beliefs.

So, what does that have to do with relieving a headache, you might ask. Not much, but everything. Not much in that they are totally unrelated results though everything in that they are both ways that the mind can produce spectacular results when freed from the restraints of our limiting beliefs. Western thinking has us believing that either over-the-counter medicine or prescribed more intense ones are the way to get rid of headaches. Please suspend those ideas for a moment and follow a simple procedure that hypnotherapists and other natural practitioners have effectively been using for ages to deal with this particular pain.

The Steps to Headache relief:

1. Find a comfortable place to sit or, preferably lie down.
2. Uncross your feet and hands and get as comfortable as possible.
3. Take some nice, deep breaths, letting them out slowly.
4. Now, on a scale from zero to 12, with 12 being the most intense, rate the intensity of your current headache.
5. After another couple of deep, relaxing breaths, picture and imaging you are in the control center of your mind and look around until you find the pain control section and more specifically, the gauge labeled "Headache Control" and notice just below it is a knob similar to the heat control on your oven and it is pointing to the number corresponding to your headache's intensity.
6. [Here is where you must suspend your belief system and just follow my directions explicitly.] As you INHALE your next breath, picture you are turning that control knob UP to the next more intense setting and feel your headache get worse.
7. Now do the same thing as you did on #6 on the next couple of breaths
8. When that pain is almost unbearable, on the next deep breath, as you EXHALE, picture and imaging yourself turning that control down one step, with a corresponding easing off of the pain.
9. Now continue taking nice slow, relaxing breaths and on the exhale, turn the intensity down one step until you reach zero and a corresponding absence of pain.

Steps #6 and 7 are the most important steps and without them this just becomes just a progressive relaxation exercise, which will probably work on its own but in a way longer time period. These steps punch through the limiting belief that we lack the ability to do anything about pains in the head other than to either suffer or to take headache relief medicines. If, when you cranked up the volume of your headache in these steps, your pain increased, your belief system automatically got an update that, by golly, you can influence the intensity of your pain. With this new belief, if you could turn it up, them of course, you can now easily turn that pain down. Without turning it up first, your inner voice would have laughed at your thinking you could just breath it down.

On occasion, I have found that my best efforts with this exercise will not relieve the pain. I finally went to the doctor and found that I had an infected sinus that was causing the pain. This exercise is not an antibiotic. If you can only succeed in dulling the pain over a period of time, it would be a good idea to find out if there was an organic cause.

True confession, here. I do sometimes rely on the Excedrin quick fix when I am too lazy or in too much of a time crunch to take the time to do this exercise.

# Relationships 101

*~ We are always in relationship with everyone in the world.
The only thing that changes is the form, and one form is
no better or worse than another, it is just different ~*

Most people, when they think of relationships make the error of viewing them in stark, black-and-white terms. They are either in a relationship full blast or they are not on speaking terms. I view relationships of all kinds, especially the more intimate of ones, in terms of shades of grey. The best concept I have found to describe this continuum of relationships is a very Eastern philosophical one. The thought is that we are always in relationship with everyone in the world. The only thing that changes is the form and one form is no better or worse than another, it is just different. Understanding that relationships are continually changing form, based on the experience of the parties to the relationship, really puts one in the mind that, to make relationships work, there needs to be good honest communication between the parties as to what is the form of the relationship at that moment.

Relationships get into trouble when one or both people have in their minds that the form of their relationship must be exactly the same as the day they met or the day they made vows of permanence, i.e.: marriage. The values of marriage have to do with sticking together through thick and thin, not attempting to hold onto a form exactly as it was on that special day. Let's face it, the couple's experience at the wedding and the assumed activities of the post wedding night will have them wake up to a slightly altered form of their relationship. Every experience they shared together from then on will have an influence on the next form of the relationship.

Sometimes the form is closer and more intimate than at other times. The couples that remain couples for the long run understand and accept that this will happen and remain in honest communication. Sometimes the experience of the couple leads them to an understanding that the form is changing to one of less contact or even no contact at all or less intimacy or no intimacy at all. If both parties recognize that this is happening and understand and accept that the form is only a reflection of their combined experience and that one form is better or worse than another one, the form at that point has the possibility of maybe changing to a less intimate one of maybe "friends" instead of one of no contact at all.

I have found in my relationships that they all started out as "just friends" and after wonderful periods of intimacy ended up again as good friends. Because we were both aware of each other's feelings as to what was going on in our interactions, when it felt like it was time to be less involved, it didn't come as a shock to either of us and we were able to make those adjustments, both physically and emotionally, to comfortably live with and in that new reality. Of course, emotions were involved though they were the emotions of change not ones of acrimony.

## The Makings of a Perfect Relationship

**"To thine own self be true"** The best relationships occur when two people, who truly love themselves and have high self-esteem, couple up. In these relationships, the partner becomes a bonus rather than a project.

All successful relationships start with and are built on a solid understanding, acceptance and love for oneself. When one or both parties enter a relationship with less than stellar self-esteem and self-love, it is a set up for failure. Such relationships are characterized by lots of fighting, manipulations and drama. The root cause of all of that is usually a partner with little self-love who is trying to suck love out of the other partner. Eventually the other partner will get tired of always being the giver and drama will ensue. If neither partner has enough esteem and love for him/herself, let alone any to share with the other partner, both will be trying to suck love out of the other who has none to give and the battles begin.

**Honesty.** Honesty is a major characteristic of successful intimate relationships (actually, all relationships). All relationships and life itself are evolutionary. The form keeps changing as the couple has more experiences together. The principle, though, is that all forms have equal value. They are just different. Even though people might prefer one form over another, their only real choice is to accept that what is, is. Refusing to accept that the form has changed, or is changing, is a primary cause of drama, grief, and bad feelings.

Honesty plays a huge role in a couple of ways. It enhances well working relationships with ongoing feedback on what is working well and what parts could be tweaked to work better. It also prevents lots of the grief and drama when the form changes to a less than intimate or engaging one. When the couple share not only what is working well but also the parts that aren't, there will be lots of opportunities to make mid-course corrections, long before the only choice of form becomes, "no contact." If they are constantly openly and honestly sharing the good and the bad aspects, it will quickly become obvious when there is a need to adjust the form (level of intimacy) to reflect the current reality. Couples that do this can usually move to a form that more resembles that of good friends or siblings rather than adversaries or having no future contact at all.

Another place where honesty and openly sharing plays a great importance is in bed. Living a life of sexual desperation because there is no conversation about what one likes or doesn't like or would love the partner to add to their sexual experience has needlessly torpedoed many otherwise great relationships. Wishing your partner would do something and expecting they

JASON WITTMAN, MPS, LAADC, CATC-IV

are mind readers is a setup for continuing frustration and lack of enjoyment. It is quite okay to occasionally give some stage directions, as well as, constructive feedback.

**There can be no blame game:** No discussion of relationships would be complete without mentioning the great role played by the way the partners view their experience of life. There are two basic views; "coming from Effect" – their experience is the effect of what people, places and things do to or for them (they are the victim), or "coming from Cause" – they recognize that how they experience life is up to them and if they do not like it they can choose an outcome or situation of their liking.

(See a complete discussion of Coming from Cause vs. Effect in the Inner Game Fundamentals section)

In relationships, one or both partners coming from effect will feature battling partners, constantly blaming each other for perceived troubles, will see themselves as victims, and if asked, will propose that the cure of the problem is for the partner to do things differently. When people come from cause, the question becomes, "what can I do differently to improve the situation" or if the situation becomes untenable, they will work on quickly removing themselves.

Knowing this, psychiatrist William Glasser, MD, incorporated it into his counseling of battling couples. In session one of two, he had the couple briefly engage in the "blame game" asking them what was wrong with the other person. Then he asked each one what they could do constructively in the following week to help repair the relationship. Then he had them commit to doing that action during the week with the instruction that if they didn't follow through, there would be no second session and they would not have to pay him anything. When they came back (all did), they reported that after they made the changes, there was more harmony.

He then instructed them to visualize three circles on the floor. He then had them each stand in a circle. He pointed out that in dysfunctional relationships, they would be standing in their respective circles telling each other about what the other needs to do to make things better. Then he had the couple move into the third, "family" circle where they each would commit to doing one thing that will help remedy the current problem, just as they had during the previous week.

One of the rules of relationships is that we can never change the other person, but we can change what we, personally, do. When each commit to making a positive change, the relationship changes from adversarial to cooperative.

**Perpetrations:** There is a subtle form of dishonesty that sometimes occurs in relationships as a more intimate form is transitioning to a less intense one. Although the tactic is quite effective in creating the change of form, the consequences of this tactic will negatively affect all future relationships of the person employing it.

The tactic is called "perpetrations" and it is a blame-shifting one. Here's how it works: One of the partners in a relationship (partner A) wants out of the current form of that relationship but does not want to openly own that desire. So partner A does something or acts in a way that causes partner B to react to which partner A uses that reaction as the reason for making the change.

Usually what happens is that partner A stops having sex for a long enough period for partner B to be horney enough to seek and have sex with a third party. When partner A catches partner B, Partner A accuses partner B of being unfaithful and enjoys a blame-free split.

The problem is that although, on the surface, it seems blame-free and actually accomplishes the detachment mission, partner

A will have acquired guilt by having not owned the desire to change the form. In most cases they won't even be consciously aware of either the perpetration process or the guilt. If it was a consciously planned perpetration, they might even feel good for having pulled this off. The problem is that it is a blatantly dishonest maneuver and for most people dishonesty is massively guilt producing. That guilt will interfere in the positive formation of future intimate relationship and when they happen will not usually last long in that form.

The most effective way to get rid of that guilt is for the perpetrator to make amends to all previous partners on which he/she pulled this stunt.

**Love Strategies**: [If you have not read the section about neuro-linguistic programming NLP 101, please do so first. It will make this discussion more understandable.]

Many folks, when they hear me talking about love strategies, will declare that they want to be spontaneous in matters of love. Communicating love is like all other communications in that it is very important that the person receiving that love communication, regardless of its form; spoken, written, or touch, unambiguously get the intended message. As with all communications, humans process them using their primary representational system, so it is very important to make sure that the love message you are sending is received as you intended it.

I make sure to understand how my partner, and for that matter, anyone important in my life, most feels being loved and appreciated. Is it getting presents, greeting cards, or flowers (visual), or being told loving messages or recorded ones on voicemail (auditory) or being hugged, holding hands, lovingly touched (kinesthetic)? The problem in many relationships where one of the partners feels that the other one does not love or appreciate as much as they would like, is that there is a mismatch of expressions of love. If, for example, partner A is visual and regularly brings home gifts and beautiful flowers but partner B processes love messages auditorily or kinesthetically, there will be a "that's nice, but does he/she _really_ love me?" All partner B needed was either a warm hug and kiss or just being told, "I love you!" to be reassured of the continuing love.

This is only one half of the story, though. The other part is to understand what _your_ love strategies are. How do you feel the most loved? Without that basic knowledge about your motivations, you will most likely express your love as you would want others to express it to you and that just might be a miscommunication. What is real interesting to me about this topic is that this love/ appreciation system is not necessarily the same as our default representational system. I am basically a visual person, yet I feel most loved when hugged, with being told, a close second. Most important is that it is critical not only to know our partner's emotional triggers but also our own. With a new partner, at sometime early in the relationship, I will purposefully do what I need to, to figure out the partner's love triggers. I will either keenly observe the reactions as I give gifts, profess my love, and hug, or if I am not able to get a good reading, I will, in a nice, casual way, ask. This is too critical for the long-term success of the relationship to be left to assumptions or chance.

By the way, all this applies to both friends and business relationships with some less intimate modifications, a warm handshake of a business associate rather than a hug, for example.

An interesting fact about hugs is that they, like all anchors, will get attached to the strongest feelings. Many long-term couples find that they stop hugging and maybe even stop touching. Much of the time, the cause can be traced back to sometime in the past, an event happened that caused the hug to be anchored to something less than pleasurable or loving. For instance, one of the partner's mother dies and the other partner in an effort to be supportive and consoling, gives his/her normal loving hug. Because of the intense grief of the moment, that hug

JASON WITTMAN, MPS, LAADC, CATC-IV

is now anchored to trauma. Moving forward to the next year when the couple is celebrating some joyous event. The partners embrace in that formerly loving hug and instead of the warm, fuzzy response from the partner whose mother died, sadness overwhelms him/her. If this happens regularly, they will stop having physical contact without knowing or understanding why and they will describe it as "the magic seems to have gone out of our relationship." How sad!

We all have a hug that is our default warm, loving hug. Mine is one arm around my partner's waist and that other hand cradling the back of the partner's neck. At times of grief or sorrow, I have a different comforting embrace of both arms around my partner's waist. Hugs, like all anchors, are very specific. I always want that warm loving hug to keep building those love feelings so I never will consciously switch to the other hug at stressful times.

## Codependency in Relationships

Many relationship problems have codependency as the root cause. My general premise is that for a relationship to work, each party needs to have so much love for his or herself that there is an excess that can then flow into the other party. What happens in relationships where the couple is regularly battling is that either one or most likely both are lacking in the self-love area. Usually, that is described as "that empty hole inside of me." In the worst-case scenario where both parties have less than adequate self-love, they are both looking to the other to "fill that empty hole." The problem is that neither of them has enough love for themselves, so they have little or none to give to the other.

People with low self-love tend to be very self-centered, "It's all about me!" They are so needy that they are constantly making demands on their partners for attention. They become very jealous when their partner pays attention to anyone else. This jealousy isn't necessarily sex-based. It can form over the partner's hanging out with old buddies. It's "but why aren't you with me?"

When this is happening on both sides of the relationship, it is easy to see how recriminations and battling can occur.

**Codependency functions as addiction:** In codependent relationships, hardly anybody leaves regardless of how heavy the conflict. To explain the reason for this, it is important to look at how codependency functions as an addiction. Whereas people with substance addictions use alcohol and drugs to deal with the hurt of little or no self-esteem and love, codependents use the attention of others for the same reasons. As with substance addictions, as long as the drug is there, the internal ache is gone. Withdraw the drug and there is an instant craving for more so as not to have to deal with the empty feelings. In the case of codependency, a person or a partner becomes the drug. As long as that other person is there, the emptiness is filled. The codependent person will do anything and everything to make sure that the other person continues to fill that need. This includes staying in very destructive relationships long after a well-functioning individual would have bailed out for self-preservation. "I know this is a lousy relationship, but it is better than nothing!" is the way a codependent mind thinks.

Codependency is one of those addictions that only becomes a problem when it crosses the line from a need to a habit. As with another one, compulsive eating, they only become problems when one switches from it being a want to a compulsive need. With overeating, it is the difference between eating to live and living to eat. In all well-functioning relationships, there is a degree of give and take where one might be giving a bit more than their level of comfortability would normally allow. Because the other party also does similar things, the payoff of having a well-functioning relationship overrides any losses, it does not cause any grief. In codependent relationships, obsessively serving the other person's needs and likes, crosses the boundary from just being a nice, supportive and loving partner to one driven by the fear of losing.

There are a number of things that are very helpful to overcome codependency. They include becoming actively involved in either/or of both Codependents Anonymous and Alanon. Alanon is a specialized niche of codependency where the partner is or was an addict or alcoholic. Both are great, supportive organizations. Alanon has been around for a long time so, especially if your partner is or was an addict or alcoholic, it would be the place where you will find the most support from folks who have been walking the walk for a long time.

Also, as with all addictions, the root cause of this one is low or no self-esteem/love/worth so for long term recovery and to prevent switching to another addiction, working on one's self-esteem and building up one's self-love is of super importance.

## Writing for Your Life

I was dragged into doing personal writing kicking and screaming all the way. Many years ago, I had a 12 Step Sponsor/mentor with whom I would meet to talk about what was going on in my life. He was someone that I called upon to assist me to sort out my current concerns.

When I would pose a problem of mine to him, he would usually reply by asking me if I had written about the problem. My reply would be no, and I just wanted to talk to him about it.

This became the regular verbal dance we did every time we spoke, until one day when he answered my question with, "I'll tell you what, I am not going to discuss this with you until you go home and write about it!" No amount of protestations would get him to budge. I was more than quite peeved, to say the least, (actually, since this is the PG version, I can only say the least).

On the way home, I stopped at my neighborhood stationery store and bought one of those 6x9 spiral notebooks and a ball point pen and, still fuming I went home and because I really wanted his advice, wrote out my problem.

After I wrote a page of "screw yuzu's!", "how dare he not talk!" and the like, I settled down to write out the original problem that I wanted to discuss with him. Lo and behold, when I was finished writing about the problem, the solution popped into my head and I didn't have to talk to him about it after all.

Little did I know when I was storming out of his house that he had just given me his best advice.

I have been writing every night before I go to bed ever since.

I journal the events of the day, my feelings about those events and my feelings at that moment about me and the other cast members in that play called "my life." It is a real taking stock type of exercise. It is an automatic writing exercise. What my mind is thinking my hand is writing. My conscious mind is an idle observer of this process. Spelling and grammar are of little importance. I do not erase or blot out anything. If something needs correcting because it was the wrong word it gets a single line through it and the pen moves on. Since I started doing this type of writing, I have found that I get to sleep faster because my mind no longer replays the day and my feelings, over and over again. For some reason, once it goes down on the paper, my mind can let go of the thought. Also, I notice that if I wrote down some problem that was of concern to me, I usually wake up with the answer. Doing this writing on a daily basis keeps me constantly in touch with my progress on the projects I am doing, allows me to fine tune the game plans to make winning more of a possibility and keeps me in touch with feelings so that there is less chance that my judgment will be clouded by them.

My strong suggestion would be to put doing nightly writing high on your "to do" list.

Many years later, I took a workshop series on "The Artist's Way: A Spiritual Path to Higher Creativity" by Julia Cameron, a seminal work for people interested in improving their creativity. Her first suggested practice is called "Morning Pages." The assignment is quite simple, write three full size notebook pages every morning with train of thought writing. That is allowing the hand to write what the brain is thinking without editing. Because I had already been writing at night for many years, I quickly embraced this practice. My fellow workshop mates really struggled with this assignment. They reported that it took them hours to finish three pages. That seemed very strange to me because I whipped them out in 45 minutes. After questioning them on how they were writing and comparing that to what I was doing, I got a grasp of the difference. That difference is the key to writing Morning Pages.

Because my Evening Writing was all about dumping my feelings, frustrations and joys of the day onto the pages, there was no reason to be creative and so I got in the habit of continuous writing until there was nothing more to write about. Along the way, I had established rules for myself concerning this writing. I did not erase or correct anything including misspellings. If it was an obvious poor choice of words, I put a line through it and continued on. The mission was to get it all on paper quickly and go to sleep.

When I started doing Morning Pages, I approached that writing the same way. My fellows were trying to craft a literary work of art, even though the author warned them not to, so they labored over every word and phrase. No wonder it took them so long! So, the take-away from this story is that when doing Morning Pages, once the pen starts writing it does not stop moving until all three pages are done! Period! If I run out of thoughts then I will describe the comfort of the pen and how smoothly the ink is flowing (I have now graduated to gel pens!), just write gibberish, or curse me out for ever committing to this exercise, but through all of that the pen does not stop.

This is an important part of doing the exercise. To understand why, we need to remember how the inner and outer minds function. Sometimes the outer mind is called the left brain or logical mind, and the inner mind the right brain, or creative one. I like the simplicity of using inner and outer minds. All creativity and exquisite action comes from the inner mind. The outer mind, when it is not busy guarding and protecting all the inner mind's operating programs, acts as the editor of all actions. It is the part that worries what other people will think, if things make sense, and if the spelling is correct. It operates in real time, meaning very slowly.

The inner mind computes at the speed of thought, a gazillion times faster than the outer mind. Any time a person is operating at their exquisite best, like a champion basketball player at the top of his game, you can bet that his outer mind is not engaged, and he is operating exclusively from his inner mind.

The same goes for writing and other creative arts. The purpose of keeping the pen moving is that it is moving faster than the outer mind can keep up with, so eventually it stops trying to, and gets out of the way. At that point pure thought and action start spilling out of the creative inner mind and onto the paper. What you are currently reading was produced exactly in this manner. Because I have been doing this practice for years, all I have to do is start writing and I am immediately in that flow of creativity.

I find that my Evening Writing and my Morning Pages are a great pair of practices. Before I go to sleep, I write my Evening Writing, in bed (use a ball-point pen, so if you fall asleep with the pen in your hand it won't drain into your sheets). That writing allows me to clear my mind of all the accumulated feelings and noise of the day. Once it is written, that infernal loop of self-talk ceases and I can get to sleep. If I have written about a problem, by morning I usually have a solution. Because my mind is clear, I get a good night's sleep so I wake refreshed and eager to see just what my inner creative mind will produce in my Morning Pages. Just like washing and showering wakes the body up, Morning Pages wakes the mind up. If you are not looking to be a writer, this exercise is still useful because it gets all the creative juices flowing and sets one up for a marvelous day!

For these reasons, I highly suggest you consider taking the advice that I did many years ago and so these writings, daily. Although you could probably alter the frequency and length of the Morning Pages and still find improvement, skipping doing the Evening Writing will affect the quality of your sleep because all those thoughts are the ones that, if not written out, will play as an eternal, infernal loop in your mind that will prevent restful sleep.

Write On!

# Conclusion

Books, and now their digital companions - the Internet and YouTube - have been how people usually get exposed to new information, how learn new ways of doing things and how to make changes in their lives. There is a built-in problem with books, though; they are always limited in the capacity to convey knowledge and be totally up to date.

Sure, it is possible to get the fundamentals from books and Internet videos and do fairly well on one's own without further assistance. The problem is that without the mentorship and guidance of those who have already walked the walk, the journey towards mastery will be tedious, longer, and probably involve wasted effort reinventing wheels. Information digested this way can introduce a subject and can even supply more detailed "how to" instruction but they will never be able to convey the tacit knowing or replace the vast experience of their writers and creators.

I read lots of Tony Robbins' writings but in no way did any of that come near to meeting the quality of the experience of working with him and getting his guidance on many occasions, as I walked through my fears, while, unscathed, I walked barefoot over 30 feet of flesh-burning wood coals! Now that is an extreme example of what I call the Moses Principle.

Moses, of biblical fame who guided the Jewish nation through the desert but was not to enter the gates of their destination with them. I believe that, in our lifetime we meet a series of moseses (small m) who walk us through a portion of our lives to the next phase where we either strike out on our own or find another mentor moses for the next part of the journey. I have had many such guides and have been in that role numerous times myself. For those of you in 12 Step recovery programs, your Sponsor is a good example.

This book was many, many years in the making. It was being written right off Professor Bronfenbrenner's words that have remained with me. I have been writing in my mind, tracking all the teachings (prescriptions) that I have repeatedly used with great success with my clients. The most frequently used ones have become this book.

If I did my job well, you ought to have a huge head start on dealing with many of the minefields that happen while on the road of a life worth living. Sometimes, though, written instructions are not enough, and it is time to find a new moses.

In a Business Law course that I took, the professor stated: The purpose of this course is to let you be able to identify where you were entering water deep enough to enlist a lawyer so to avoid needing a more painful rescue. It is not to turn you into business lawyers.

So it is with all of life. I am confident that if you read this book and practice the lessons I have presented, you will be able to navigate most of life's stuff. For the rest, I and professional folks like me, are here to be your next moses. And as my professor said, it is much better to recognize where it is time to get a guide to navigate deeper water than to wait to need rescuing.

I still do have a limited private practice. If you are interested in working with me, all my contact information is on my website, http://Stage2Recovery.com For as long as I am capable of answering email and picking up a phone, I will.

JASON WITTMAN, MPS, LAADC, CATC-IV

In the Resources Section you will find a listing of the books that have been my best guides, both professionally and personally and links to other useful resources,

For an ever increasing, and up to date resource guide, check out the digital version on my website, http://Stage2Recover.com/resources or https://bit.ly/jasonwrecommends

My guiding principles are these: Life is a journey, a series of digressions and progressions. There is no destination other than to keep on with creating a life worth living. Take time to stop and occasionally appreciate the magic of a rosebud growing or a starlit sky. Remember, there is not a shred of evidence that life is supposed to be serious. Smile!

# About the Author

Jason Wittman has both his B.S. degree in business management and a Master's in Counseling Psychology from Cornell University. He is a Certified, Level IV, Addictions Counselor, an Internationally Certified Clinical Supervisor, and has been a life, mentor, and sober coach since the early 1980s.

In a private practice as a Counselor and Coach since the middle 1980s, he focuses on coaching and advising business and professional clients, who are recovering from alcoholism and addictions to work and live at their exquisite best. He specializes in the enhancement of self-esteem/love, the lack of which is the root cause of all addictions and most everything else.

He has assisted countless clients walk through the trials, tribulations, and joys of their lives: Hollywood celebs that needed assistance with stage fright and with the fears and hassles that quick success and fame can bring; executives on how to better work and communicate with their employees and bosses; parents of Teens and Young Adults teaching and coaching effective parenting. Jason's coaching has been credited with being the critical factor that allowed them to successfully walk through difficult personal relationships and transitional times in their lives. He has an ability to intuitively know the "rest of the story." That and his skill as a certified hypnotherapist and Neuro-Linguistic Practitioner serves his clients well. Because he coaches the "inner game," he is regularly called on to assist clients who are having problems with getting their insides, their self-esteem, in sync with their high-performing, high self-confident outsides.

As pioneer in the recovery field, Jason career started in 1971, when, while still in grad school, he founded and ran a residential therapeutic community for drug addicts and alcoholics. He has been counseling and coaching people in varying stages of recovery and in many different therapeutic settings ever since.

He has a limited private practice. If you are interested in working with him, all his contact information is on his website, http://Stage2Recovery.com

# Suggested Books and Readings of Interest
to People interested in Creating a Life Worth Living

(When possible, I have linked the title of the books below with Amazon.com so that you can easily acquire them at a reasonable price. I would appreciate if you would use these links. Although it won't affect the book price in any way, Amazon will know I referred you and will thank me with an infinitesimally small monetary token of their appreciation.)

**Join my Facebook Group** Most books like mine, that I have read, usually left lots of questions that I would have loved to have asked the author and couldn't. Well, this author has always believed that my relationship with my clients and readers was an ongoing and evolving one based on their needs and what they felt I could contribute to their making their life's journey better. To that end, I have created an exclusive Facebook Group for you to be able to ask those questions that come up from applying what you read to your life and get answers from me as well as from other group members. You can join at: https://www.facebook.com/groups/663645381379447

**Stage II Recovery: Life Beyond Addiction** by Earnie Larsen. This is the book for people who have been in recovery long enough to have worked the Steps through, at least once, and who are ready to deal with the rest of their lives now that substance abuse and addictions are no longer the issues. Definitely a companion book to my coaching. https://amzn.to/2WZomlb

**Stage II Relationships: Love Beyond Addiction** by Earnie Larsen. In the same mode as Stage II Recovery but in this book, he takes that one chapter on relationships and gives it a full book treatment. Another companion to my relationships coaching. https://amzn.to/3ngWmEq

**Napkin Notes on the Art of Living** by G Michael Durst, Ph.D. The best self-help book on the market!" is the summation for all of the five-star ratings on Amazon. Although countless self-help books have been written, none have been able to translate psychological theory into practical, day-to-day application as well as this one does. By integrating Eastern and Western philosophy with science and religion, Napkin Notes provides a concise, easy-to-read guide for living. Dr. Durst promotes the concept that we are 100% responsible for everything in our experience and for our reactions to life's events. This focus provides not only increased knowledge, but also the impetus to change. In so doing, it directs us to greater insight, satisfaction, and fulfillment. https://amzn.to/3yQu0CU

**Actualizations: You Don't Have to Rehearse to Be Yourself** by Stewart Emery Stewart Emery was one of the first people to lead EST training, and one of the founders of Actualizations, a supportive and loving workshop that helps people establish joyful relationships in their lives. The purpose of this book is to provide the groundwork for a complete transformation of its reader's relationships—into sources of joy, satisfaction, and exhilarating personal growth. The philosophy described here will allow you to deepen not only your connection with others, but your understanding of yourself. Emery's *Actualizations* will allow you to live life to its fullest—no reservation, or rehearsal, required! https://amzn.to/3ttivA5

**Choice Theory: A New Psychology of Personal Freedom** by William Glasser, M.D. Dr. Glasser offers a new psychology that, if practiced, could reverse our widespread inability to get along with one another, an inability that is the source of almost all unhappiness.

For progress in human relationships, he explains that we must give up the punishing relationship; destroying external control psychology. For example, if you are in an unhappy relationship right now, he proposes that one or both of you could be using external control psychology on the other. He goes further. And suggests that misery is always related to a current unsatisfying relationship. Contrary to what you may believe, your troubles are always now, never in the past. No one can change what happened yesterday. https://amzn.to/3jTGoh3

**Counseling with Choice Theory** by William Glasser, M.D. In *Counseling with Choice Theory,* Dr. William Glasser takes readers into his consulting room and illustrates, through a series of conversations with his patients, exactly how he puts his popular therapeutic theories into practice.

These vivid, almost novelistic case histories bring Dr. Glasser's therapy to life and show readers how to get rid of the controlling, punishing *I know what's right for you* psychology that crops up in most situations when people face conflict with one another.

Practical and readable, *Counseling with Choice Theory* is Dr. Glasser's most accessible book in years. https://amzn. to/3hhQuXv

**Getting Together and Staying Together: Solving the Mystery of Marriage** Dr. Glasser and his wife Carleen co-wrote this book. Using the Choice Theory principles, they build a great life together which they told me had been fight-free since they were married. They stayed a happy couple until Dr. Glasser's death. https://amzn.to/2Yu2PRN

**When The Shoe Fits: Stories of the Taoist Mystic Chuang Tzu** by Osho (Bhagwan Shree Rajneesh) This is one of my favorite practical philosophy books. *"Only that which is attained through effortlessness will never be a burden to you."* That is the message of the renowned Indian philosopher Osho, one of the 10 people (others include Gandhi, Nehru, and Buddha) said to have changed the very destiny of his nation.

This previously little-known study—a true classic of interpretation—presents his distinctive and highly illuminating exploration of Taoism. Osho offers penetrating commentary on the stories of Chinese philosopher Chuang Tzu, the tradition's founder, as well as inspirational anecdotes on the quest for love, spiritual understanding, and true happiness. The powerful combination of Taoist wisdom and Osho's insightful interpretation make this a true gem, appropriate for the growing audience interested in Eastern thought. https://amzn. to/3EaDDAm

**Influencing with Integrity: Management Skills for Communication and Negotiation** by Genie Z. Laborde, Ph.D. Dr. Laborde is one of the original group of folks surrounding the founders of NLP and who was very involved in the foundational work of NLP. This book was the first one to apply the NLP framework and techniques to business communication and management. https://amzn.to/3l0GCSU

**The Parent as Coach Approach** by Diana Sterling, - Parents: Are you having problems with your teenager? Tired of constant conflict, struggle, attitude, miscommunication, and chaos in your home? Are you overwhelmed and frustrated with crazy-making behavior and teenage antics? This is THE handbook! If you are in any country and there are teens present - GET THIS BOOK NOW!!! Professionals: Are you looking for a handbook that is easy to read for your parent and family clients? Here is the ONE you have been waiting for! COACH YOUR CLIENTS FROM THIS BOOK WITH PARENTS OF TEENS AND TEENS, PRE-TEENS AND YOUNG ADULTS! I personally know Diana as a colleague, and this is the book that I use when teaching parenting to parents of teens. https://amzn.to/3ngfimz

The next four books are the most wonderful books to explain some of the fundamental personal and intrapersonal issues. They are mainly comic-style illustrations with commentary. They are a valuable resource for folks of all ages:

**The Facade: A View of Ourselves** by Jim Cole. The Facade is an expression of the sharing of ourselves and the risking of ourselves with others. It looks at the resistance to risk taking and the joys that come from being known and sharing one's self with another.

This book is very simple yet seems to hold some personal truths for many people. https://amzn.to/3l7nWB5

**Helpers: A View of Our Helpfulness** By Jim Cole. The Helpers looks at our motives for behaving both helpless and helpful and then examines what effects these motives have on ourselves and on those we try to help. It expresses the helplessness of trying to help others. It then examines how we often escape these helpless feelings and what this does to us and those we are trying to help. https://amzn.to/38Qx1sj

**The Controllers: a view of our responsibility** by Jim Cole, The Controllers is a look at freedom and responsibility for one's own behavior. It explores how escaping the responsibility for one's behavior often results in loss of freedom. It explores the fear and the loneliness that comes with feeling free and responsible. This cartoon book has been used with both alcoholics and juveniles for many years. https://amzn.to/38PzqDt

**Filtering people: A view of our prejudices** by Jim Cole An excellent tool for workshops, courses, and personal reflection, Filtering People: Understanding and Confronting Our Prejudices gently and sympathetically helps us identify our prejudices, explore how and why we become prejudiced-and learn how we can begin to overcome our prejudices. Filtering People enriches our lives by helping us see each other as we are, in all our fascinating diversity. Filtering People has been used widely and avidly by people trying to understand, confront and change prejudices. https://amzn.to/3BVMVOI

Real Boys and Real Boys Handbook by William S Pollack, Ph.D

**Real Boys: Rescuing Our Sons from the Myths of Boyhood by William S. Pollack, Ph.D.** Based on William Pollack's groundbreaking research at Harvard Medical School over two decades, Real Boys explores this generation's "silent crisis": why many boys are sad, lonely, and confused although they may appear tough, cheerful, and confident. Pollack challenges conventional expectations about manhood and masculinity that encourage parents to treat boys as little men, raising them through a toughening process that drives their true emotions underground. Only when we understand what boys are really like, says Pollack, can we help them develop more self-confidence and the emotional savvy they need to deal with issues such as depression, love and sexuality, drugs and alcohol, divorce, and violence. https://amzn.to/3mXGG8m

**Real Boys Workbook : The Definitive Guide to Understanding and Interacting with Boys of All Ages** by William S Pollack, Ph.D and Kathleen Cushman The Real Boys' Workbook is a unique, instructive workbook, full of advice, exercises, and stories to help parents, professionals, and boys themselves understand boys—and how to make life with them better. How to listen to boys, talk and be with them, exercises to teach you new ways to handle situations, and strategies for coping with problems (drug and alcohol abuse, gender identity, depression, bullies) are addressed, as readers are encouraged to respond to questions and situations, to learn how to think about boys with new understanding, and to react more creatively. Through writing down responses in the workbook, using the charts and summaries, and taking part in the provocative question-and-answer sections, you will gain insight into boys and their problems and be better able to be with them in effective and powerful ways. https://amzn.to/308AQsl

**Frogs into Princes** by Richard Bandler, Ph.D. and John Grinder, Ph.D. "Frogs Into Princes" three-part introduction to NLP (short for "Neuro Linguistic Programming"), a form of therapy conceived of in the 1970s. NLP is founded on the premise that "the kinds of problems that people have usually have nothing to do with content; they have to do with the structure, the form of how they organize their experience." (47) The central thesis of NLP, then, is that the best way to help others overcome emotional, behavior, and psychosomatic problems is to discern the processes by which they organize and access their thoughts and feeling and alter it. https://amzn.to/3wu94Cc.

**The Street Shrink Chronicles** by Jason Wittman, MPS is fond of saying, "All teens and young adults deserve 24/7 access to at least one responsible, caring adult who loves them unconditionally." Unfortunately, many teens get cut off from their families and end up on the streets fending for themselves. For the past thirty-five years, Jason has been a father figure to countless teens and young adults.

Follow Jason as he deals with street violence, suicides, judges, and cops. Be there as hopelessly lost kids begin to turn around their lives as they receive his attention and guidance. With a mixture of high drama, raw dialogue, and tender moments, that novel capture what it is like to work with street kids on their turf.

Loosely based on his real-life experiences working with kids living on their own, Jason captures the essence of what it takes to work those miracles for which he has become renowned. https://amzn.to/3l4wXeh

I am regularly adding to this list on my website. Check there for the latest additions. http://stage2recovery.com/suggested-readings/ or https://bit.ly/readlst

[Please note: Any book or program that I am recommending is one that I either read, use and/or know well enough to put my credibility behind the suggestion. Some of these referrals might give me a small monetary gift as a thank you. Rest assured that my referral cannot be bought and I only list what I can stand behind and where what you have to invest is either the same or less than if you ordered directly.]

©2019 - 2022, Jason Wittman, MPS, LAADC, CATC-IV
http://Stage2Recovery.com
jason@s4mm.com

# A GENTLE, LAST REMINDER

Hopefully, you have already downloaded the eBook.
If not, Scan this QR Code for a special and
personal message from Jason.
And a bonus, 45 page "deep-dive" eBook

Or go to:
http://wittmanent.groovepages.com/offer